IRELAND
AND THE
LOW COUNTRIES
1575-1825

By David Dobson

CLEARFIELD

Published for Clearfield Company by
Genealogical Publishing Company
Baltimore, Maryland
2025

ISBN: 9780806360676

CONTENTS

Ireland and the Low Countries, 1575-1825

INTRODUCTION

Since the early medieval period, Ireland has experienced invasion and settlement from abroad. The most notable invasions include the Norse Vikings from around 850 AD, the Anglo-Normans under Strongbow (alias Richard Fitzgilbert de Clare) in 1170, and the English under King Henry II in 1171, and under the Tudors in the late 16th and 17th centuries.

The English initially settled in the south-east of Ireland but gradually expanded their power throughout much of the island. The Tudor English struggled with the native Irish until the end of the Nine Years War in 1604, and the "Flight of the Earls" to France or Flanders. King James then allocated their lands among "undertakers" who undertook to settle immigrants from Scotland and England in the Plantation of Ulster. Rebellions against Cromwellian rule in Ireland, such as the Confederate Wars of 1641-1652, led to confiscation of rebel lands, which the Crown granted to former soldiers and to those who had financed the military. Though the Jacobite forces of King James consisted, in part, of French soldiers, and those of King William were partly Dutch and French, there is no sign of their settlement in Ireland at that time.

The Low Countries, especially the cities of Rotterdam, Amsterdam, Antwerpen, Ostende, and Brugge, were major markets for goods and raw materials imported from Asia, Africa, and the Americas. The continuous stream of ships bound for or returning from the Low Countries encouraged Irish merchants to settle there. Low Countries universities, such as the University of Leiden, attracted Irish scholars. Most of the Irish migrants in Flanders or elsewhere in the Netherlands arrived as soldiers, some in Spanish service, others in English or Dutch service. Irishmen such as Owen Roe O'Neill, Thomas Preston, and Garret Barry, who had experienced warfare in Flanders and in the Thirty Years War, were among those soldiers who returned to Ireland to fight with their Catholic Confederates in their struggle with the forces of the English Parliament. During the Wars of the Three Kingdoms (alias the English Civil War), the indigenous Irish sided with the King, since Parliament was anti-Catholic. This led to Irish and Flemish privateers, like John O'Daniel of Limerick (and formerly in Dunkirk and Ostend), now being based at Waterford or Wexford attacking English or Parliamentary ships.

King Charles II took refuge in the Netherlands after being defeated at the Siege of Worcester in 1651. After his restoration to the thrones of England and Ireland in 1660, he encouraged the settlement of Protestants from the Netherlands and Flanders, as well as French Huguenots, in Ireland. On 23 August 1661, King Charles II approved of a bill naturalising Dutch and other Protestant strangers "for there are now many Protestants in France, Flanders, and other parts that are industrious people, that if they might be there naturalised, would come over and bring with them persons skilled in making several sorts of manufactures." On 7 September 1661, the Earl of Orrery wrote to Secretary Nicholas "it did my heart good to see at Limerick forty Dutch families, which I had lately gotten thither so busy in their manufactures and plantations." Flemish Huguenots, in particular, settled in centers such as Dublin, Cork, Youghal, Port Arlington, and at Lisburn.

David Dobson
Dundee, Scotland, 2025

REFERENCES

ABR Aberdeen Burgh Records

ACL Aberdeen Council Letters

AGS Archivo General de Simancas, Spain

AH Archivum Hibernicum

BL British Library, London

BMF Belfast Merchant Families, [Dublin 1996]

CSPDom   Calendar of State Papers, Domestic

CSPIre Calendar of State Papers, Ireland

CTB Calendar of Treasury Books

FLJ   Finn's Leinster Journal

IC Ireland under the Commonwealth, [Manchester, 1913]

IPR Irish Patent Rolls

IS Irish Sword, [Dublin]

LHL   Linen Hall Library, Belfast

MM Mariners Mirror, series

NRS National Records of Scotland, Edinburgh

ONA Old Notarial Accounts, Rotterdam

PRONI Public Record Office of Northern Ireland, Belfast

RA Rotterdam Archives

SH Studio Hibernica, Dublin.

SM Scots Magazine, series

SPDom State Papers, Domestic

SPIre State Papers, Ireland

TCD Trinity College, Dublin

Transatlantic Lives, [Belfast, 2019]

TNA The National Archives, London

UL University of Leiden

UU University of Utrecht

WG Wild Geese in Spanish Flanders, 1582-1700, [Dublin, 1964]

w of the b...

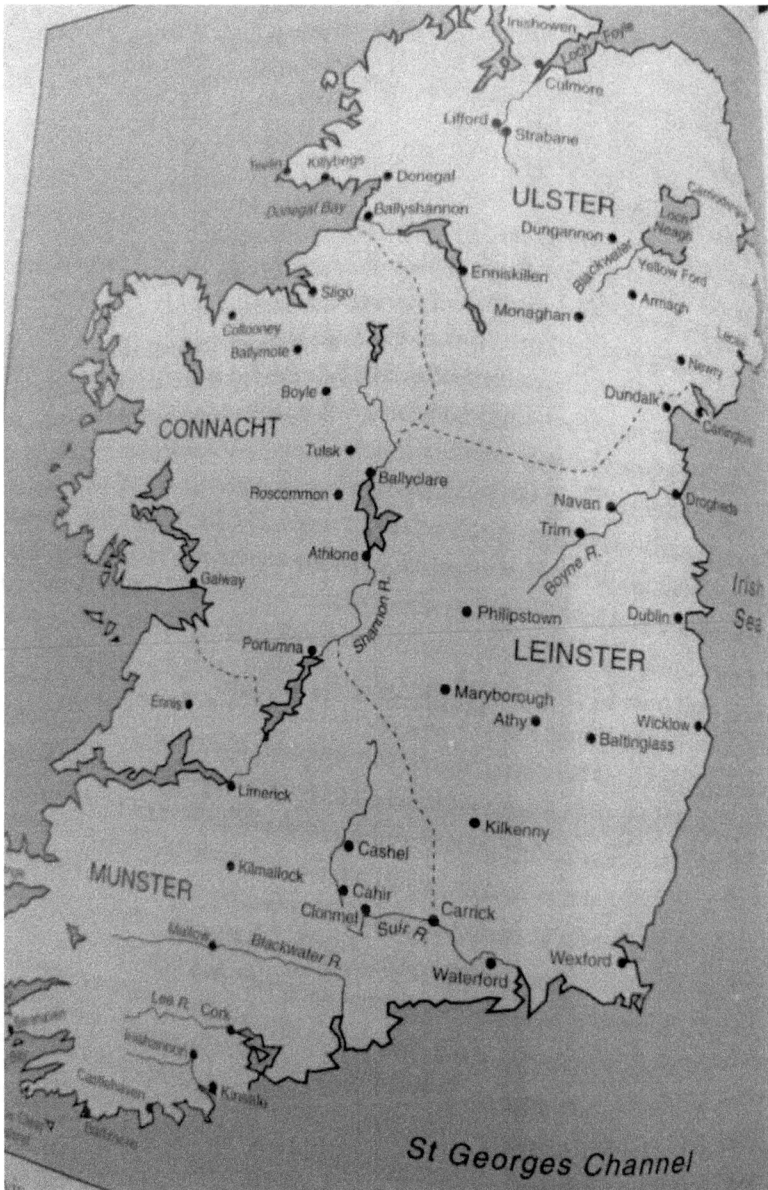

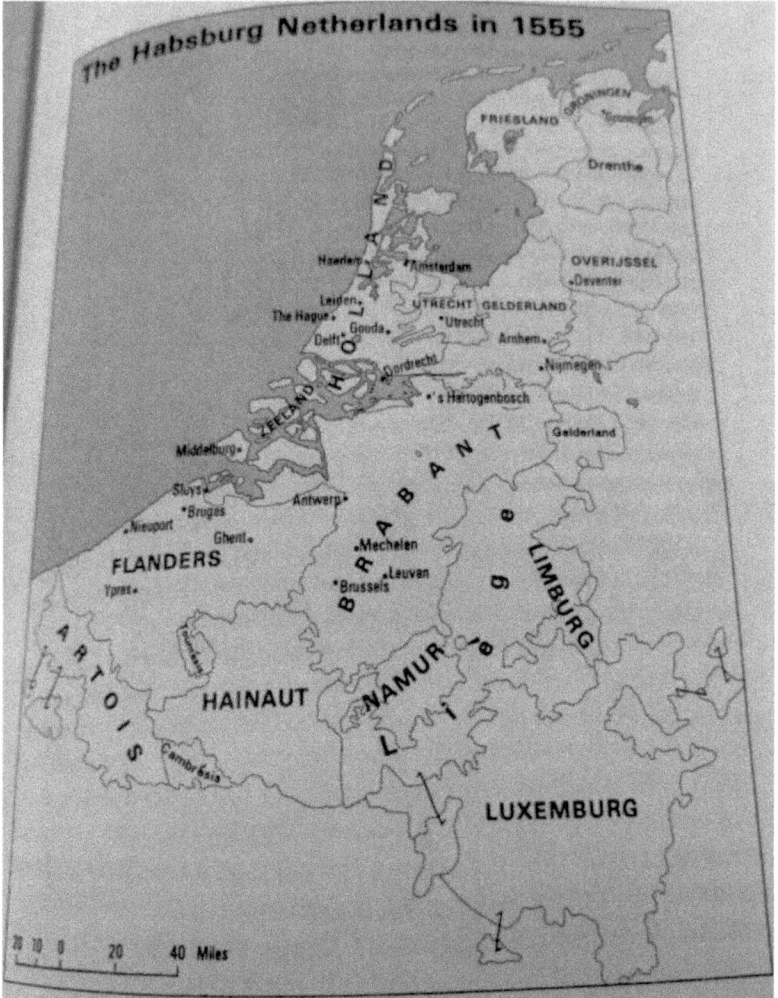

The Habsburg Netherlands in 1555

FRIESLAND
GRONINGEN
Drenthe
HOLLAND
Haarlem
Amsterdam
OVERIJSSEL
Deventer
Leiden
UTRECHT GELDERLAND
The Hague
Gouda
Utrecht
Delft
Arnhem
Dordrecht
Nijmegen
ZEELAND
's Hertogenbosch
Middelburg
Gelderland
Sluys
B R A B A N T
Nieuport
Bruges
Antwerp
L i m b u r g
Ghent
Mechelen
LIMBURG
FLANDERS
Brussels
Leuven
Ypres
A R T O I S
HAINAUT
NAMUR
L i è g e
Cambrésis
LUXEMBURG

20 10 0   20   40 Miles

x

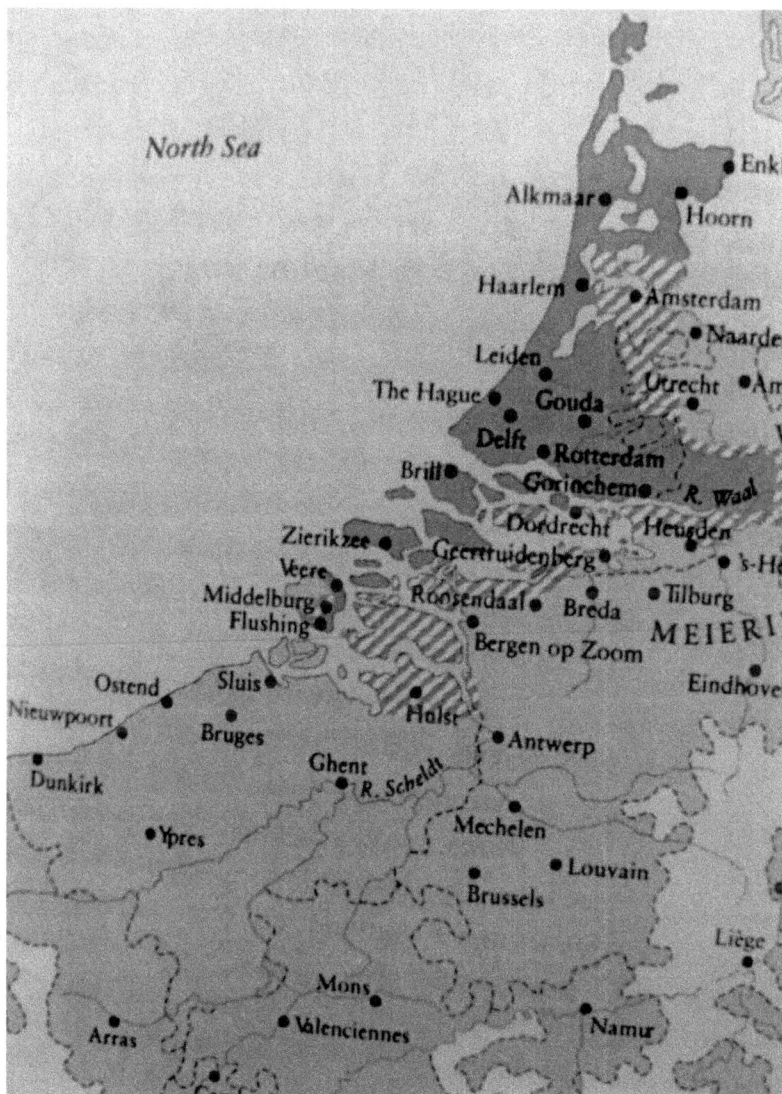

North Sea

Enk[l]
Alkmaar
Hoorn
Haarlem
Amsterdam
Naarde[r]
Leiden
The Hague
Gouda
Utrecht
Am[...]
Delft
Rotterdam
Brill
Gorinchem
R. Waal
Dordrecht
Heugden
Zierikzee
Geertuidenberg
's-H[...]
Veere
Middelburg
Roosendaal
Breda
Tilburg
Flushing
Bergen op Zoom
MEIERI[...]
Ostend
Sluis
Eindhove[n]
Nieuwpoort
Hulst
Bruges
Antwerp
Dunkirk
Ghent
R. Scheldt
Ypres
Mechelen
Louvain
Brussels
Liège
Mons
Valenciennes
Namur
Arras

Irish Soldiers

5ᵀᴴ ROYAL IRISH DRAGOONS
DISBANDED - 1798.
1742   1751   1751

ADAIR, ROBERT, born in 1716, an Irish student at the University of Leiden in 1742. [UL]

ADRIANS, DANIEL, from the Netherlands was denizised in Ireland on 1 February 1640. [IPR]

ADRIANS, HIBERT, from the Netherlands was denizised in Ireland on 1 February 1640. [IPR]

ADRIANSON, PETER, from Strien in the Netherlands was denizised in Ireland on 1 February 1640. [IPR]

AITON, ROBERT, an Irish academic at the University of Leiden in 1696. [UL]

ALLERT, JAN, steersman aboard the Angel Raphael bound from Amsterdam to Limerick in 1648, was examined by the High Court of the Admiralty of England in 1650. [TNA.HCA.30.659]

AMALRY, J. S., in Rotterdam, a letter to Robert Percival in Dublin, dated 16 March 1785. [PRONI.D906.288]

AMIA, ELIAS, born 1621, a merchant from Haarlem in Holland but residing in Dublin a witness in 1645. [TNA.HCA.13.58.165/166]

ANCKETILL, OLIVER, a student at Utrecht University in 1704. [RCPE]

ANDERSON, JOHN, born 1708, an Irish student at the University of Leiden in 1734. [UL]

ANTHONY, JOHN, in Amsterdam, a letter to John Bradshaw in Belfast dated 23 December 1760. [PRONI.D354.628]

ANTHONY, JOHN, CROSS, and Company in Amsterdam, reference to in a letter dated 24 July 1755. [PRONI.D353.765]

ARCHDEACON, HENRY, from Cork, was admitted as a citizen of Rotterdam on 7 December 1752. [RA]

ARCHDEACON, JOHN, born 1628, a merchant in Ross, and servant of Richard de la Haye there, The Prince Christian of Copenhagen had sailed from Middelburg with a cargo of hops, madder and tobacco for Thomas de la Haye and Lucas Le Croy merchants in Ross but was captured by a Parliamentary ship and taken to Bristol. [TNA.HCA.13.61.271]

ARCHER, JAMES, SJ, from Kilkenny, a military chaplain to Sir William Stanley's Regiment in Flanders around 1587. [SI.30.122]

ARCHER, ROBERT, born 1690, an Irish student at the University of Leiden in 1714. [UL]

ARCHIBALD, PATRICK, born 1703, an Anglo-Irish student at Leiden University in 1724. [UL]

ARCHIBOLD, PETER, Judge Advocate of Taafe's Irish regiment in the Low Countries from 1672 until 1673, also Judge Advocate of Colonel Denis O'Byrne's Irish Regiment in the Low Countries from 1673 until 1686. [WG]

ARIENS, JOHN, born 1602, master of the Oak of Heusden in Holland, from Waterford with a cargo of hides, wool, books, and stockings, when bound for Amsterdam was captured by Captain Bedell of the Adventure in 1647. The ship was owned by John Ebbs, Lanc Hempson, and other merchants in Amsterdam. [TNA.HCA.13.62.345]

ARNIA, ELIAS, a Dutch merchant residing in Dublin around 1645. TNA.HCA.13.60]

AUDMAN, MICHAEL, an Anglo-Irish academic at the University of Utrecht in 1699. [UU]

AYLMER, ANTHONY, a Captain of Colonel Thomas Preston's Irish Regiment in Flanders from 1634 until 1641. [WG]

BAILLIE, JOHN, born in 1702, an Irish student at the University of Leiden in 1728. [UL]

BAILLIE, WILLIAM J., from Ireland, married Annetie Negenduysent on 7 August 1695 in the Scots Church in Rotterdam. [RA]

BAKER, THOMAS, who trained as a book-keeper in Ostend became an Agent of the Burlington Estate in Ireland in 17.... [NAI.222]

BAKKER, CREESYE, reference to in will of Abel De Le Deveze, probate 1749. [PCC]

BAKKER, GEORGE, reference to in the will of Abel De Le Deveze, in 1749. [PCC]

BAL, JOHN, an Irish infantryman in Brussels in 1591. [AGRB.45]

BALLANTINE, JAMES, from Dublin, was admitted as a citizen of Rotterdam on 22 April 1747. [RA]

BARBER, CONSTANTINE, born in 1714, an Irish student at the University of Leiden in 1738. [UL]

BARDON, ..., a Lieutenant of MacElligott's Regiment in Flanders around 1688. [IS]

BARING, F., in Amsterdam, a letter to Earl MacCartney dated 16 September 1794. [PRONI. D.572.19.172]

BARNABAL, VALENTINE, a Captain of Colonel Charles Dillon's Regiment bound for Flanders in 1653. [WG]

BARNEWALL, ALEXANDER, a Lieutenant of MacElligott's Regiment in Flanders around 1688. [IS]

BARNEWELL, Captain PATRICK, of MacElligott's Regiment in Flanders around 1688. [IS]

BARNEWELL, SIMON, a Lieutenant of MacElligott's Regiment in Flanders around 1688. [IS]

BARON, LAURENCE, born 1618, of Ostend, master of the John Baptist of Waterford when bound from Oostende [Ostend] with a cargo of muskets, holsters, pistols, woollen cloth, flax, tobacco and iron, despatched by Irish factors in Flanders destined for Browne and Stephens merchants in Waterford was captured by John Bowen master of the Hart in November 1648. [TNA.HCA.13/61.209/305]

BARRET, JOHN, born in Cork in 1717, an Irish student at the University of Leiden in 1737. [UL]

BARRET, WILLIAM, Captain of Colonel Henry O'Neill's Irish Regiment in Flanders in 1605. [WG]

BARRY, DAVID, from Cork, married Ann Sprie, a widow, in a Presbyterian Church in the Netherlands on 8 November 1702.

BARRY, EDWARD, born 1696, an Irish student at Leiden University in 1718. [UL]

3

BARRY, Colonel GARRET, a veteran of the Spanish Army in Flanders, was appointed as Commander of the Confederate forces in Munster, fought at the Siege of Limerick in 1642.

BARRY, GERALD, a Captain of Colonel John O'Neill's Regiment in Flanders from 1610 until 1628. [WG]

BARRY, JAMES, an Ensign of Colonel Patrick O'Donnell's Irish Regiment in Flanders from 1643 until 1647. [WG]

BARRY, NICHOLAS, a Sergeant of Colonel John O'Neill's Regiment in Flanders from 1610 until 1628. [WG]

BARRY, NICHOLAS, a Captain of Colonel Theodore O'Meara's Irish Regiment in the Low Countries from 1660 to 1664. [WG]

BARRY, RICHARD, an Ensign of Colonel John Morphy's Irish Regiment in Flanders from 1646 until 1659. [WG]

BARRY, WILLIAM, chaplain of Colonel Henry O'Neill's Irish Regiment in Flanders in 1605. [WG]

BATH, PATRICK, a Captain of Colonel James Dempsey's Irish Regiment in the Low Countries from 1660 until 1662. [WG]

BAYLY, PAULUS, from Dublin, was admitted as a citizen of Rotterdam on 30 June 1718. [RA]

BAYNAM, JOHN, an Irish soldier of Colonel Stanley's Regiment in Brussels in 1590. [AGRB.28]

BEACH, RICHARD, master of the Michael of Wexford captured the Three Blackmores of Flushing in August 1648 [TNA.HCA.13.249]

BEAGHAN, CORNELIUS, an Irish student at the University of Leiden in 1733. [UL]

BEDELL, THOMAS, master of the Adventure captured the Angel Gabriel in February 1649 when bound from Amsterdam to Limerick. [TNA.HCA13.249]

BEECH, THOMAS, master of the Shadwell from Dublin bound for Rotterdam and Bruges, then return via Weymouth to Dublin in 1689. [CTB.IX.100]

BELL, GEORGE, born 1690, an Irish student at the University of Leiden in 1712. [UL]

BELLORE, MARINUS, a seaman from Vlissingen, [Flushing] was denisized in Ireland on 6 September 1671. [IPR]

BENGALL, ADRIAN, a master mariner from Middleburg was denisized in Ireland on 10 November 1671. [IPR]

BENNET, EDWARD, born 1685, an Irish student at Leiden University in 1707. [UL]

BERMINGHAM, NICHOLAS, a Captain of Colonel John Morphy's Irish Regiment in Flanders from 1646 until 1659. [WG]

BERMINGHAM, RICHARD, an Ensign of Colonel John Morphy's Irish Regiment in Flanders from 1646 until 1659. [WG]

BERN, CHARLES, a Captain of Colonel Theodore O'Meara's Irish Regiment in the Low Countries from 1660 to 1664. [WG]

BERNARD, FRANCIS, a Captain of Colonel Charles Dillon's Regiment bound for Flanders in 1653. [WG]

BERNIVAL, FRANCIS a Captain of Colonel John Morphy's Irish Regiment in Flanders from 1646 until 1659.[WG]

BERTIN, PETER, a Captain of Colonel James Dempsey's Irish Regiment in the Low Countries from 1660 until 1662. [WG]

BESNARD, PIETER, toured Ulster in 1823 promoting the Dutch method of flax cultivation. [PRONI.D207.28]

BLACK, JOHN, from Ireland, married Maetge Thyssen from Rotterdam, on 23 March 1635. [RA]

BLACK, JOHN, from Ireland, married Pleasant Parker from England, in the Netherlands on 26 January 1642.

BLAIR, LAMBERT, born in Newry, a merchant and slave trader in St Eustatia, Dutch West Indies by 1779.

BLOCK, ADRIAN, master of De Liefde Van Vlissingen from La Rochelle, with a cargo, sent by Richard Butler an Irish merchant in France, of salt, liquorice, aniseed, res, starch, copper, tobacco and vinegar bound for Richard De La Hay in Ross, via Dublin but was captured by Captain Gilson of the Constant Warwick, a Parliamentary ship, and taken to Plymouth on 27 August 1647. Passengers were James Furlong of Danesfort in Ghent, John Bourk of Bennetsbridge, Arthur Browning of Rathcoole, and Edmond Eustace from Dublin. [TNA.HCA.13.248.606/609/610]

BLOUCABLE, Captain, master of the Bonaventure van Vlissingen, was captured in April 1665 at sea and taken to Kinsale, Ireland, where the ship was sold to Thomas Gookin, a merchant there, on 20 July 1665, while the crew were imprisoned in Cork. [SPIre.1663-1665, 665]

BOCTIUS, CORNELIS, from Ireland, married Lysebet Aerians from Dordrecht on 19 July 1598.

BOELL, WILLIAM, from Antwerpen in Brabant, was denizised in Ireland on 11 June 1607. [IPR]

BOLLARDT, ABIGAIL, died 1656, daughter of John Bollardt, a merchant in Antwerp, and wife of Ridgely Hatfield the Mayor of Dublin. [DPR.232]

BOLTON, Captain CORNELIUS, from Waterford, died in Ghent, Flanders, probate. 1700. Prerogative Court of Canterbury. [TNA]

BOLTON, THOMAS, born 1693, an Irish student at Leiden University in 1714. [UL]

BONBONE, PETER, born 1712, an Irish student at the University of Leiden in 1732. [UL]

BOR, CHRISTIAN, from the Netherlands, was denizised in Ireland on 1 May 1618. [IPR]

BOR, CORNELIUS, from Dublin, a student at Utrecht University in 1655. [RCPE]

BOR, JOHN, from the Netherlands, was denizised in Ireland on 14 May 1618. [IPR]

BOSGEL, PATRICK, a soldier from Ireland, found guilty of theft from Leiden in Holland on 9 November 1621. [PL.54]

BOSMAN, JOHN, master of the Phoenix of Flushing [Phoenix van Vlissingen] was captured by Thomas Plunkett, master of the Discovery in 1645. [TNA.HCA.13/248]

BOSTOCK, ROBERT, Captain of an Irish Regiment, was sent to support the Dutch against the Spanish from 1586 until 1587 when the regiment changed allegiance in favour of Spain until 1604. [WG]

BOULTON, Captain CORNELIUS, from Waterford, residing in Ghent in Flanders, probate 1700, Prerogative Court of Canterbury. [TNA]

BOURT, DAVID LUCAS, from Ireland, married Jannet Jan on 13 February 1656. [RA]

BOUWIER, JAMES, born 1695, an Irish student at the University of Leiden in 1735. [UL]

BOYLE, HENRY, from Castlemartyr in County Cork, died in Ghent, Flanders, 1694, Prerogative Court of Canterbury. [TNA]

BOYS, EDWARD, formerly a midshipman aboard HMS Phoebe, 'a narrative of capture and adventures in France and Flanders between 1703 and 1709'. [NLI].

BOYS, WILLIAM, a Lieutenant of MacElligott's Regiment in Flanders around 1688. [IS]

BOYES, THOMAS, master of the Gift of God of Aberdeen when bound from Aberdeen to Veere in June 1639 was captured by an Irish frigate and taken to Ireland. [ACL.2.378]

BOYLE, CORNELIUS, born 1712, an Irish Student at the University of Leiden in 1735. [UL]

BOYLL, NELAN, an Ensign of Colonel John O'Neill's Regiment in Flanders from 1610 until 1628. [WG], he as an Ensign of Captain Bruin's company of the Earl of Tyrone's Regiment, was sent to Ireland in 1632 to recruit a company for the Earl of Tyrconnell. [AGRB.1197]

BRADY, JOHN, Adjutant of Colonel Philip O'Reilly's Irish regiment in the Low Countries from 1655 until 1660. [WG]

BRADY, PHILIP, an Ensign of Colonel James Dempsey's Irish Regiment in the Low Countries from 1660 until 1662. [WG]

BRAMHALL, JOHN, Anglican Bishop of Londonderry, later Archbishop of Armagh a Royalist in exile in Brussels in 1640s. [ODNB]

BRANGAN, MARTIN, Ensign of Colonel Henry O'Neill's Irish Regiment in Flanders in 1605. [WG]

BRANN, HENRY, master of the Ormond of Dublin from Barbados bound for Holland in 1669. [CSPIre]

BRAPTSON, EDWARD, born 1709, an Irish Student at the University of Leiden in 1734. [UL]

BREMIGAN, EDMUND, a Captain of Colonel John Morphy's Irish Regiment in Flanders from 1646 until 1659. [WG]

BRENACH, CHARLES, an Adjutant of Colonel Denis O'Byrne's Irish Regiment in the Low Countries from 1673 until 1686. [WG]

BRETT, IGNATIUS, master of the frigate Patrick of Wexford a privateer which was captured by the President master Nathaniel Fearns, in 1649. [TNA.HCA13.58.834]

BRETT, THOMAS, a Sergeant Major who died in Ireland, probate 1599, Prerogative Court of Canterbury. [TNA]

BREYN, DIMES, from Cork, married Grittle Willems Brouwer from Rotterdam, in Rotterdam on 15 March 1705. [RA]

BRIDGES, EDWARD, from Cork, was admitted as a citizen of Rotterdam on 2 April 1735. [RA]

BRON, VALENTINE, Quartermaster of Colonel John O'Neill's Regiment in Flanders, from 1610 until 1628. [WG]

BRONOK, THOMAS, born in 1724, an Irish student at the University of Leiden in 1744. [UL]

BRONTVELD, CATHARINA, from Dublin, married Jacobus Kandnk from London, in the City Church in Rotterdam on 9 August 1753. [RA]

BROOK, HENDRIK, from Limerick, was admitted as a citizen of Rotterdam on 9 June 1749. [RA]

BROUWE, JOHN, in Ostend, factor for Joshua Allen a merchant in Dublin around 1666. [LHL.Macartney Letter Book]

BROWNE, JAMES, from Zealand, a resident of Dublin, was denizised in Ireland on 29 December 1622. [IPR][DPR.244]

BROWNE, PATRICK, born in 1716, an Irish student at the University of Leiden in 1743. [UL]

BROWN, ROBERT, in Utrecht, a letter to Sir George MacCartney, dated 2 October 1770. [PRONI.D572.3.138]

BROWN, WILLIAM, born 1684, a Scots-Irish student at Leiden University in 1708. [UL]

BROWN, WILLIAM, born 1686, a British-Irish student at Leiden University in 1710. [UL]

BRUEN, HERMAN, master of the Three Blackamores of Flushing, 5 guns, was captured by the privateer Michael of Wexford, in 1648. [TNA.HCA.13.249]

BRUM, OLIVER, a Sergeant of Colonel John Morphy's Irish Regiment from 1646 until 1659. [WG]

BRUN, AMBROSE, an Adjutant of Colonel John Morphy's Irish Regiment in Flanders from 1646 until 1659; a Captain of Colonel Theodore O'Meara's Irish Regiment in the Low Countries from 1660 to 1664. [WG]

BRYANT, HUMPHRY, waiter aboard the Mercurius van Vlissingen [Mercury of Flushing] was imprisoned in Cork in 1665. [SPIre.1663-1665]

BRYCE, EDWARD, born in 1722, an Irish student at the University of Leiden in 1744. [UL]

BRYTH, ALEXANDER, a Captain of Colonel Theodore O'Meara's Irish Regiment in the Low Countries from 1660 to 1664. [WG]

BUCKLE, JOHN JOHNSON, from Ireland, married Lysbet Jacobs from Rotterdam on 27 August 1715. [RA]

BUCKLY, RICHARD, from Clonwell in Ireland, married Isobel Robertson, from Belfast, Ireland, in Rotterdam on 11 January 1758. [RA]

BUDARD, COLARD, master of the Sant Pieter van Vlissingen [St Peter of Flushing], was captured when bound from Ostende to Dublin or Waterford in December 1647. [TNA.HCA.13.60]

BURKE, DAVID, an Irish soldier in Colonel William Stanley's Regiment at Bergen op Zoom on 17 October 1588. [AGRB.10]

BURKE, DAVID, an Adjutant of Colonel James Dempsey's Irish Regiment in the Low Countries from 1660 until 1662. [WG]

BURKE, EDMOND, an Ensign of Colonel O'Donnell's Irish Regiment in Flanders from 1643 to 1647. [WG]

BURKE, JOHN an Irish soldier in Colonel William Stanley's Regiment at Bergen op Zoom on 17 October 1588. [AGRB.10]

BURKE, JOHN, an Adjutant of Colonel John O'Neill's Regiment in Flanders, from 1610 until 1628. [WG]

BURKE, JOHN, a chaplain of Colonel Patrick Fitzgerald's in Flanders from 1639 until 1641. [WG]

BURKE, JOHN, a Captain of Colonel Hugh O'Donnell's Regiment in Flanders from 1632 until 1638. [WG]

BURKE, JOHN, an Ensign of Colonel John Morphy's Irish Regiment in Flanders from 1646 until 1659. [WG]

BURKE, JOSEPH, born in 1698, an Irish student at the University of Leiden in 1738. [UL]

BURKE, LEWIS, a Captain of Colonel DenisO'Byrne's Irish Regiment in the Low Countries from 1673 until 1686. [WG]

BURKE, RICHARD, an Irish soldier in Colonel William Stanley's Regiment at Bergen op Zoom on 17 October 1588. [AGRB.10]

BURKE, RICHARD, a Captain of Colonel Owen Roe O'Neill's Irish Regiment in Flanders from 1633 until 1642. [WG]

BURKE, RICHARD, an Ensign of Colonel Denis O'Byrne's Irish Regiment O'Byrne's Irish Regiment in the Low Countries from 1673 until 1686. [WG]

BURKE, THEOBALD, a Captain of Colonel John Morphy's Irish Regiment in Flanders from 1646 until 1659; a Captain of Taafe's Irish Regiment in the Low Countries from 1672 until 1673. [WG]

BURKE, THOMAS, a Captain of Taafe's Irish Regiment in the Low Countries from 1672 until 1673; a Captain of Colonel Denis O'Byrne's Irish Regiment in the Low Countries from 1673 until 1686. [WG]

BURKE, WALTER, an Irish soldier in Colonel William Stanley's Regiment at Bergen op Zoom on 17 October 1588. [AGRB.10]

BURKE, WALTER, an Ensign of Colonel John Morphy's Irish Regiment in Flanders from 1646 until 1659. [WG]

BURKE, WILLIAM, an Irish soldier in Colonel William Stanley's Regiment at Bergen op Zoom on 17 October 1588. [AGRB.10]

BURNE, PATRICK, an Ensign of MacElligott's Regiment in Flanders in 1688. [IS]

BURNE, TIMOTHY, Captain of MacElligott's Regiment in Flanders around 1688. [IS]

BURNEN, ROBERT, from Ireland, married Adrientje Kennedy, the widow of Cornelis Makoen from Ireland in Rotterdam on 19 February 1651. [RA]

BUSHEL, ESTER, from Dublin, married James De Spomare, in the Scots Kirk in Rotterdam on 12 July 1725. [RA]

BUTLER, EDMOND, a Captain of Colonel Hugh O'Donnell's Regiment in Flanders from 1632 until 1638. [WG]

BUTLER, EDWARD, a Captain of Colonel Patrick Fitzgerald's Regiment in Flanders from 1639 until 1641. [WG]

BUTLER, EDWARD, a Captain of Colonel James Dempsey's Irish Regiment in the Low Countries from 1660 until 1662; Captain of Colonel John Murphy's Irish Regiment in the Low Countries from 1667 until 1669; a Captain of Colonel Denis O'Byrne's Irish Regiment in the Low Countries from 1673 until 1686. [WG]

BUTLER, JAMES, from Dublin, married Catherina Ver Meulen from 'Den Bosch in the Reformed Church in Rotterdam on 18 March 1687. [RA]

BUTLER, PETER, Major of Colonel John Morphy's Irish Regiment in Flanders from 1646 until 1659. [WG]

BUTLER, PETER, a Captain of Colonel James Dempsey's Irish Regiment in the Low Countries from 1660 until 1662. [WG]

BUTLER, RICHARD, a Captain of Colonel John O'Neill's Regiment in Flanders from 1610 until 1628; a Captain of Colonel John Morphy's Irish Regiment in Flanders rom 1646 until 1659. [WG]

BUTLER, THEODORE, an Ensign of Captain Shaa's Company of Colonel Louis Farrell's Irish Regiment in the Low Countries around 1660. [WG]

BUTLER, THOMAS, an Irish soldier at the Siege of Alost in 1585. [AGRB.3]

BUTLER, THOMAS, a Captain of Colonel Owen Roe O'Neill's Irish Regiment in Flanders fro 1633 until 1642. [WG]

BUTLER, WILLIAM, a Captain of Colonel Owen Roe O'Neill's Irish Regiment in Flanders from 1633 until 1642. [WG]

BUTTER, ANTHONY, an Ensign of Colonel George Cusack's Regiment in the Low Countries from 1656 until 1662. [WG]

BUYS, CHRISTIAAN, from Dublin, was admitted as a citizen of Rotterdam on 9 November 1740. [RA]

BYLE, ADRIAN, steersman of the Fortune of Amsterdam from the Texel to Kinsale in November 1649. [TNA.HNC.13.251]

BYRCH, HENRY, from Dublin, a student at Utrecht University in 1669. [RCPE]

CADEL, WILLIAM, of Colonel Stanley's Regiment at Spa in 1589. [AGRB.16]

CAHILL, HUBERT, a Chaplain of the Earl of Bristol's Irish Regiment bound for the Low Countries in 1657. [G]

CAIRNES, JOHN, born 1684, an Irish student at Leiden University [AH.59] [UL]

CAIRNS, THOMAS, born 1675, a Scots-Irish student at Leiden University in 1704. [AH.59] [UL]

CAIRNES, THOMAS, an Irish academic at the University of Utrecht in 1705. [UU]

CAIRNES, THOMAS, an Irish student at the University of Utrecht in 1705. [UU]

CALENHOOSEN, Reverend Andres, the Dutch minister, and his wife Rachel, referred to in the will of Nicholas Rohd in St Mary's, Dublin, dated 22 April 1708, Dublin.

CALLAGHAN, ..., a chaplain of Colonel Patrick Fitzgerald in Flanders from 1639 until 1641. [WG]

CALLAGHAN, JOHN, a chaplain of Colonel Owen Roe O'Neill's Irish Regiment in Flanders from 1633 until 1642. [WG]

CALLAGHAN, JOHN, from Waterford, was admitted as a citizen of Rotterdam on 10 November 1793. [RA]

CALLAGHAN, WALTER, a Captain of Colonel Owen Roe O'Neill's Irish Regiment in Flanders from 1633 until 1642. [WG]

CAMPBELL, JOHN, born 1680, an Irish student at Leiden University in 1701. [AH.59][LU]

CAMPBELL, JOHN, a Scots-Irish student at the University of Utrecht in 1705. [UU]

CANT, CHARLES, a mariner in Rotterdam, master of the Blessing of Amsterdam, [Bidden van Amsterdam] from Amsterdam via Wales, Ireland, and return in 1645, was captured in June 1645 by Richard Swanley, master of the Lion. In June 1645 the Blessing then in Dublin was loaded with hides, the property of Daniel Wybranson to be transported to him and Isaac Paulson in Amsterdam or Rotterdam.
[TNA.HCA.13.60/161/247]

CARD, SAMUEL, born 1707, an Irish student at Leiden University in 1725. [UL]

CAREW, JOHN, a Captain of Colonel Thomas Preston's Irish Regiment in Flanders from 1634 until 1641. [WG]

CARLY, THEODORE, a Captain of Colonel John Morphy's Irish Regiment in Flanders from 1646 until 1659. [WG]

CARR, GEORGE, a Captain of Colonel Thomas Preston's Irish Regiment in Flanders from 1634 until 1641. [WG]

CARR, WILLIAM, born 1673, an Anglo-Irish student at the University of Leiden in 1696. [UL]

CARROLL, JOHN, an Ensign of Colonel Theodore's Irish Regiment in the Low Countries, from 1660 until 1664. [WG]

CARROLL, PATRICK, a Sergeant of Colonel James Dempsey's Irish Regiment in the Low Countries from 1660 until 1662. [WG]

CARSTAIRS, ALEXANDER, in Rotterdam insured the Friendship from Killybegs, Donegal, Ireland, to Barbados in 1705, also the Hopewell in 1706. [PRONI.D501.1]

CARTHY, FLORENCE, an Ensign of Colonel Patrick Fitzgerald in Flanders from 1639 until 1641; an Ensign of Colonel John Morphy's Irish Regiment in Flanders from 1646 until 1659. [WG]

CARTY, DANIEL, a Captain of Colonel Patrick, O'Donnell's Irish Regiment in Flanders from 1643 to 1647; a Captain of Colonel John Morphy's Irish Regiment in Flanders from 1646 until 1659. [WG]

CARTY, DENIS, Ensign of Colonel Henry O'Neill's Irish Regiment in Flanders in 1605. [WG]

CARTY, DERMOT, a Captain of Colonel Patrick O'Donnell's O'Donnell's Irish Regiment in Flanders from 1643 to 1647. [WG]

CARTY, DERMOT, a Captain of Colonel Patrick O'Donnell's Irish Regiment in Flanders from 1643 to 1647. [WG]

CARTY, FELIX, a Sergeant of Colonel John Morphy's Irish Regiment from 1646 until 1659. [WG]

CARTY, JAMES, a Captain of Colonel Patrick Fitzgerald's Regiment in Flanders from 1639 until 1641. [WG]

CARTY, THADEUS, Captain of Colonel Henry O'Neill Irish Regiment in Flanders in 1605; later Captain of Colonel Patrick O'Donnell's Irish Regiment in Flanders from 1643 to 1647. [WG]

CARTY, THADEUS, an Ensign of Colonel Patrick O'Donnell's Irish Regiment in Flanders from 1643 to 1647. [WG]

CARTY, THADEUS, a Captain of Colonel Dermot O'Sullivan's Irish Regiment in Flanders, from 1646 until 1647. [WG]

CARVEL, DENIS, from Ireland married Neeltje, from Amsterdam, in the Reformed Church of Rotterdam on 31 May 1654. [RA]

CARWELL, BARNABUS, an Irish academic at Utrecht University in 1712. [UU]

CASSIDY, HUGH, chief surgeon of Colonel James Dempsey's Irish Regiment in the Low Countries from 1660 until 1662. [WG]

CATHERWOOD, JOHN, an Irish student at the University of Utrecht in 1710. [UU]

CAVANAGH, BERNARD, a Captain of Colonel Theodore O'Meara's Irish Regiment in the Low Countries from 1660 to 1664. [WG]

CAVANAGH, GREF, a Captain of Colonel Thomas Preston's Irish Regiment in Flanders from 1634 until 1641. [WG]

CAVERLIN, JOHN, a Lieutenant of MacElligott's Regiment in Flanders around 1688. [IS]

CAWS, HENRY, a Captain of Colonel John Morphy's Irish regiment in Flanders from 1646 until 1659. [WG]

CHAIGNEAU, JEAN, from Dublin, was admitted as a citizen of Rotterdam on 17 June 1762. [RA]

CHELAN, ROBERT, from Ireland, was admitted as a citizen of Rotterdam on 16 March 1771. [RA]

CHORTAL, PETER, a Captain of Colonel James Dempsey's Irish Regiment in the Low Countries from 1660 until 1662. [WG]

CHRISTIAN, ABRAHAM, a merchant from Middelburg in Zealand, was naturalised in Ireland on 31 December 1667. [BL.Egerton.77][IPR]

CHRISTOPHER, CORNELIUS, from Zealand, residing in Dublin, was denizised in Ireland on 29 December 1622. [IPR]

15

CHUSLER, JONATHAN, reference to in will of Abel De Le Deveze, in 1749. [PCC]

CLAARE, WILLIAM, from Waterford, was admitted as a citizen of Rotterdam on 18 June 1714. [RA]

CLANCY, MORAGH, a Captain of Colonel James Dempsey's Irish regiment in the Low Countries from 1660 until 1662. [WG]

CLANSAM, WILLIAM, from Stembergen in the Netherlands, was denizised in Ireland on 29 January 1920. [IPR]

CLARKE, SAMUEL, from Belfast, was admitted as a citizen of Rotterdam on 13 October 1728. [RA]

CLASON, DERRICK, from Stavarn in Friesland, purser aboard the Angel Raphael of Copenhagen bound from Amsterdam to Limerick in 1648, was examined by the High Court of the Admiralty of England in 1648. [TNA.HCA.30.649; HCA.13.249]

CLEMENT, CORNELIUS, master of the White Greyhound of Middelburg with its crew of twenty-three men, were captured at sea and taken to Kinsale, County Cork, where the Dutch ship was sold to Edmund Yeomans, a merchant there, for £260 on 19 July 1665. [SPIre.1663-1665.665]

CLERY, DENIS, a chaplain of Colonel Patrick Fitzgerald in Flanders from 1639 until 1641. [WG]

CLERSON, MARY, born 1632, from Dunkirk, Flanders, sailed from Waterford aboard the Angel Gabriel bound for France but storm-damaged put into Swansea in Wales during 1650. [TNA.HCA.30.853]

CLIGNETT, JOHN, from Aachen, was denizised in Ireland on 28 February 1663. [IPR]

CLOYSON, CLOYS, master of the Bordeaux van Vlissingen when bound from the West Indies for Waterford was captured by William Penn, master of the Assurance in January 1647. [TNA.HCA13/62]

COCHETEUX, ANTHONY, a shoemaker from Comen, Flanders, was naturalised in Ireland on 9 March 1665. [BL.Egerton.7]

COELL, NICHOLAS PIETERSON, born in the Netherlands, was denizised in Ireland on 15 July 1624. [IPR]

COESTGLAN, FRANCIS, a Captain of Colonel John Morphy's Irish Regiment in Flanders from 1646 until 1659. [WG]

COESTGLAN, TERENCE, a Captain of Colonel John Morphy's Irish Regiment in Flanders from 1646 until 1659. [WG]

COGHLAN, LAURENCE, Adjutant of Taafe's Irish Regiment in the Low Countries from 1672 until 1673. [WG]

COGHLAN, MORIAT, a Captain of Colonel John Morphy's Irish Regiment in Flanders from 1646 until 1659. [WG]

COGLON, TERENCE, a Captain of Colonel John Morphy's Irish Regiment in Flanders from 1646 until 1659. [WG]

COLLET, CLAUDE, master of the privateer St Joseph of Wexford captured the Martin van Vlissingen at the Ile de Re in April 1648.

COLLIS, JOHN, an Ensign of Colonel Johnston's Regiment at Ostend, Flanders, probate 1745, Diocese of Ardfert and Aghadoe.

COLLIS, WILLIAM, born 1694, an Irish student at the University of Leiden in 1714. [UL]

COMERFORD, JOHN, a Captain of Colonel Thomas Preston's Irish Regiment in Flanders from 1634 until 1641. [WG]

CONNEL, DAVID, born 1702, an Irish student at the University of Leiden in 1736. [UL]

CONNELL, JOHN, from Cork, was admitted as a citizen of Rotterdam on 1 December 1739. [RA]

CONNELL, TERENCE, a Sergeant of Colonel James Dempsey's Irish Regiment in the Low Countries from 1660 until 1662. [WG]

CONNINGHAM, JAMES, from Londonderry, was admitted as a citizen of Rotterdam on 9 January 1737. [RA]

CONNOCK, Captain WILLIAM, of MacElligott's Regiment in Flanders around 1688. [IS]

CONNOR, DENIS, of Colonel Stanley's Regiment at Spa in 1589. [AGRB.16]

CONNOR, THEODORE, an Ensign of Colonel Theodore's Irish Regiment in the Low Countries, from 1660 until 1664. [WG]

CONRAGEN EWAN, a Sergeant of Colonel Dermot O'Sullivan's Irish Regiment in Flanders, from 1646 until 1647. [WG]

CONRON, ARTHUR, from Ireland, was admitted as a citizen of Rotterdam on 17 April 1748; in Rotterdam, a letter to Daniel Mussenden dated 1 October 1756. [PRONI.D354.625] [RA]

CONROY, JULIUS, a Doctor of Colonel Owen Roe O'Neill's Irish Regiment in Flanders from 1633 until 1642. [WG]

CONSTANTINE, DERMOT, a Captain of Colonel Patrick O'Donnell's Irish Regiment in Flanders from 1643 to 1647. [WG]

CONTENT, JOSEPH, born 1619, from Dunkirk master of the privateer St Peter of Waterford, a privateer which captured many, mostly, English ships some were then sent as prizes to Waterford or Ostend. The St Peter was captured by the Parliamentary frigate Phoenix off Portland, England, in July 1649. [TNA.HCA.15.2.840]

CONWAY, JAMES, born in 1718, an Irish student at the University of Leiden in 1741. [UL]

CONYNGHAM, Captain WILLIAM, in Osnaburg, a letter to Lord Pembroke in Utrecht dated 13 April 1782. [PRONI.D1440.12.82]

COPE, HENRY, born 1684, an Irish student at Leiden University in 1708. [UL]

COPPAGE, RICHARD, born 1699, an Irish student at Leiden University in 1719. [UL]

CORNELIUS, ANTONIUS, master of the Mercurius van Vlissingen, [Mercury of Flushing] which was captured at sea and taken to Kinsale, County Cork, where it was sold to Robert Cooke, a merchant in Youghal, County Cork, for £430 in July 1665, while the crew was imprisoned in Cork in May 1665. [SPIre.1663-1665.]

CORNELIS, JAN, from Ireland, married Tryntje Barents, in the Reformed Church in Rotterdam on 21 July 1613. [RA]

CORNELISON, BOREN, master of the Rommelenhaven van Hoorn, was captured in September 1648 by the frigate Warwick, master John Edwyn when bound from Limerick to Hoorn in Holland. [TNA.HCA23/15]

CORNELISON, GARRET, master of the Oranjeboom van Amsterdam when bound for Waterford, was captured in October 1645 by John Hosier, master of the Magdalen in October 1645. [TNA.HCA13.60]

CORNELSON, RICHARD, master of the Fortuin van Amsterdam from the Texel, Holland, to Kinsale, County Cork, in November 1649. [TNA.HCA.13.251]

CORNELISSON, ADRIAN, born in Holland, was naturalised in Ireland on 22 December 1618. [IPR]

CORNELISSON, WYBRANS OCKER, born in Holland, was naturalised in Ireland on 22 December 1618. [IPR]

CORRY, JAMES, born 1681, an Irish student at Leiden University in 1701. [AH.59][UL]

COSBY, PETER, born 1701, from Ireland, was a student at Leiden University in 1721. [UL]

COSTELLO, DUDLEY, Colonel of an Irish regiment in the Low Countries from 1653, later served in Lorraine. [WG]

COUGHLAN, CORNELIUS, born 1632 in Limerick, a seaman resident in Ostende, Flanders, since 1630, he was a seaman aboard the John the Baptist of Waterford which was seized by the frigate Hart when sailing from Ostende to Waterford, Ireland, in 1648. [TNA.HCA.13.61]

COUGHLAN, FRANCIS, a Captain of Colonel George Cusack's regiment in the Low Countries from 1656 until 1662. [WG]

COURTNEY, JOHN, from Ballynery in County Armagh, enlisted in the Royal North British Fusiliers 1745, but was transferred to the Scots-Dutch Brigade, from which he deserted to the French then enlisted into the 'Regiment de Berwick' at Alost. [JSA.406.187][HR. 101]

COXGLAN, MAURICE, a Captain of Colonel John Morphy's Irish regiment in Flanders from 1646 until 1659. [WG]

19

COYMAN, JACK, a merchant in Dublin, a deed in the Rotterdam Archives in 1648. [ONA.Rotterdam.482]

CRAIGH, JAMES, from Limerick, was admitted as a citizen of Rotterdam on 29 June 1709. [RA]

CRAMER, BALTHAZAR, from Geesin, Upper Germany, was denizised in Ireland on 29 January 1620. [IPR]

CRAWFORD, JAMES, in Rotterdam, a letter to A. Stewart and Company, refers to a Mr Haanwinckel, dated 25 November 1726. [PRONI.D654.B2.96]

CREAGH, ANDREW, was born in Cork, lived in Amsterdam for ten years, settled in Virginia in 1652. [TNA.HCA.13.68]

CREAGH, CHARLES, a Captain of Colonel Philip O'Reilly's Irish regiment in the Low Countries from 1655 until 1660; a Captain of Colonel John Morphy's Irish regiment in Flanders from 1646 until 1659. [WG]

CREAGH, PATRICK, from Limerick, sent the St Peter from Amsterdam to Nantes, France, in 1653, a factor or merchant in Vlissingen [Flushing] around 1670. [TNA.HCA.13.68] [BMF.181]

CREAMER, TOBIE, from the Netherlands, was denizised in Ireland on 28 May 1639. [IPR]

CRISPIN, ANTHONY, boatswain aboard the Oyster Hoyle [?] of Rotterdam, shipped a cargo of tobacco etc, to Galway for Oliver French a merchant there in 1648. [TNA.HCA.30.855]

CROES, DAVID, a merchant from Guelderland, in the Netherlands, was naturalised in Ireland on 14 October 1664. [BL.Egerton.77][IPR]

CROFT, MAURICE, a chaplain of Colonel Patrick O'Donnell's Irish Regiment in Flanders from 1643 to 1647. [WG]

CROFTON, EDWARD, born 1687, an Irish Student at the University of Leiden in 1737. [UL]

CROKER, THOMAS, born 1695, an Irish student at Leiden University in 1714. [UL]

CROLL, EGIDIUS, senior and junior, from the Netherlands, were denizised in Ireland on 1 December 1619. [IPR]

CROL, GILES, a merchant in Ireland, a deed in the Rotterdam Archives in 1621. [ONA.Rotterdam.78/108/226]

CROND, ROBERT, from Charlemont in Ireland, married Margaret Richardson from Scotland, in the Reformed Church of Rotterdam on 18 January 1702. [RA]

CRONE, DANIEL, a cutler from Troylson in Pomerania, was denizised in Ireland on 14 October1663. [IBR]

CRONING, CORNELIUS, master of the London van Flissingen [Flushing in Holland], when bound from La Rochelle with a cargo of salt, tobacco, four, aqua vita, biscuits, etc, for merchants in Waterford, namely Alexander Sherlock, Bennett White, Richard Hoare, Michael Cransten, Nicholas Grant, Francis Hoare, James Shea, Peter De Frize, and Edward Browne, was captured by the Nunsuch, Captain Richard Willoughby, on 31 January 1649. [TNA.HCA.15.2.897]

CROOSE, REMENS, master of the Sampson van Flissingen [Sampson of Flushing] in August 1646 when bound from Limerick. [TNA.HCA13/60]

CROWLEY, THOMAS, born 1707, an Irish student at the University of Leiden in 1747. [UL]

CRUMP, GEORGE, born 1694, an Irish student at Leiden University in 1714. [UL]

CUDMORE, MICHAEL, a student at Utrecht University in 1699. [RCPE]

CUERK, MICHAEL, a Sergeant of Colonel Patrick O'Donnell's Irish Regiment in Flanders from 1643 to 1647. [WG]

CUIN, WALTER, an Irish soldier at Spa in 1589. [AGRB.15]

CUL, THOMAS, a Sergeant of Colonel Patrick O'Donnell's Irish Regiment in Flanders from 1643 to 1647. [WG]

CULLRICUS, JOHN, of Alumbe in Germany, formerly Commander of a Company in the Service of the Duke Wilhelm of Saxe-Weimar, a passenger aboard the Fortune of Dunkirk from Dunkirk bound for Ireland in May 1643 to seek his fortune. [TNA.HCA.13.246.507]

CUNNINGHAM, JOHN, from Dublin, was admitted as a citizen of Rotterdam on 10 November 1793. [RA]

CURTIS, JOHN, born in 1717, an Irish student at the University of Leiden in 1737. [UL]

CUSACK, CHARLES, an Ensign of Colonel Denis O'Byrne's Irish Regiment in the Low Countries from 1673 until 1686. [WG]

CUSACK, GEORGE, Colonel of an Irish Regiment in the Low Countries from 1656 until 1662. [WG]

CUSACK, PETER, an Ensign of Colonel George Cusack's Regiment in the Low Countries from 1656 until 1662. [WG]

CUSACK, RICHARD, a Sergeant of Colonel John Morphy's Irish Regiment in Flanders from 1646 until 1659. [WG]

CUSACK, RICHARD, Captain of Colonel John Murphy's Irish Regiment in the Low Countries from 1667 until 1669; an Adjutant of Colonel Denis O'Byrne's Irish Regiment in the Low Countries from 1673 until 1686. [WG]

CUSACK, ROBERT, a Captain of Colonel Theodore O'Meara's Irish Regiment in the Low Countries from 1660 to 1664. [WG]

CUSACK, Colonel, an Irish soldier in Flanders around 1665. [CSPIre]

DALL, SARA, from Dublin, married Hendrik Beeking from Delshaven in Rotterdam on 12 May 1805. [RA]

DALTON, NICHOLAS, a Captain of Colonel Owen Roe O'Neill's Irish Regiment in Flanders from 1633 until 1642; a Captain of Colonel Patrick O'Donnell's Irish Regiment in Flanders from 1643 to 1647. [WG]

DALTON, WALTER, a Captain of Colonel Hugh O'Donnell's Regiment in Flanders from 1632 until 1638. [WG]

D'ALTON, Count EDWARD, of Grenanstown, County Tipperary, Colonel of Clairfait's Regiment of Foot and a Lieutenant Colonel in Austrian Service, was killed at the Battle of Hoondscoote near Dunkirk, Flanders, in 1793. [Bath Abbey gravestone]

DALY, JOHN, master of the Unity of Cork was captured when bound from St Malo in Brittany to Cork and taken to Salcombe in 1642. [TNA.HCA.13.58.4]

DALY, JOHN MICHAEL, born 1725, an Irish student at the University of Leiden in 1750. [UL]

D'AMOUR, JOHN, a merchant from Amsterdam in Holland, was denizised in Ireland on 18 April 1670. [IPR]

DAMUCH, CHRISTOFFER, a hodman from Ireland, married Maertgen Robertsdaughter, widow of William Adas, in Leiden in Holland, during November 1638. [Leiden Marriage Register]

DANCKERT, CHRISTIAN JACOB in Cork, probate 1787, Diocese of Cork and Ross.

DANIEL, JOHN, an Irish soldier of Colonel Stanley's Regiment in Brussels in 1590. [AGRB.29]

DANIEL, JOHN, born in Ireland, master of the Paul of Dunkirk took refuge in the Royalist port of Dartmouth to escape capture by Parliamentary ships in 1645. [TNA.HCA.23.29.154]

DANIEL, PATRICK, a Major of Colonel Owe Roe O'Neill's Regiment in Flanders from 1633 until 1642. [WG]

DANIEL, ROBERT, Captain of Captain Henry O'Neill's Irish Regiment in Flanders in 1605. [WG]

DANIEL, WILBERT, a merchant from Vlissingen in Zealand, was naturalised in Ireland on 18 January 1669. [BL.Egerton.77]

DANIELSON, GEORGE, master of the Lemon Tree of Middelburg, trading from Galway to Middelburg in Holland in 1651. Exports, comprising fleece wool, tallow, furs, and hides, by merchants in Galway – John Power, Andrew Creagh, John Whitt, Francis Creagh, John Bodkin, Thomas Lynch, Patrick Creagh Fitzdavid, Daniel Arthur, also a merchant in Limerick – William Creagh, for Thomas Lynch and Andrew Creagh, merchants in Middelburg. [TNA.HCA.15.5.847]

DARBY, NATHANIEL, from Dublin, was admitted as a citizen of Rotterdam on 29 September 1733. [RA]

DARCY, GERALD, Ensign of Colonel Henry O'Neill's Irish Regiment in Flanders in 1605. [WG]

DARCY, WILLIAM, Captain of Colonel Henry O'Neill's Irish Regiment in Flanders in 1605. [WG]

23

DARGAN, WILLIAM, Captain of Colonel John Murphy's Irish Regiment in the Low Countries from 1667 until 1669. [WG]

DARRAGH, JOHN, from Dublin, was admitted as a citizen of Rotterdam on 16 November 1756. [RA]

DAUBRIE, RICHARD, a student at Louvain University inn1633. [RCPE]

DAVEY, JOSEPH, born in 1707, an Irish student at the University of Leiden in 1727. [UL]

DAVEY, WALTER, from Londonderry, was admitted as a citizen of Rotterdam on 3 November 1740. [RA]

DAVIDSON, ANN, from Dublin, married John Beggs from Newcastle, England in the Presbyterian church in Rotterdam on 23 March 1707. [RA]

DAVIDSON, JAMES, a mariner from Breda in Brabant, was naturalised in Ireland on 13 December 1669. [BL.Egerton.77][IPR]

DAVIDSON, WILLIAM, from Cork, was admitted as a citizen of Rotterdam on 13 June 1709. [RA]

DE CROSSE, EMANUEL, in Middelburg, Zeeland, loaded the Prince Christian of Copenhagen, master Anders Petersen, born 1608 in Copenhagen with cargo bound from Veere to Ross and Waterford in January 1648, in Ireland his factor and brother
Lewis de Crosse loaded hides, wool, tallow etc bound for Veere but was taken to Bristol by a Parliamentary ship the Expedition.
[TNA.HCA.13.58.274/275]

DE GEER, LAURENCE, now resident in Amsterdam, and Abraham van Hogaerden, formerly in Limerick, late in partnership in Ireland, whose assets were seized by the king as de Geer was classed as an alien enemy, 24 May 1666. [SP.Ire.1666.115]

DE HAES, GABRIEL, from Antwerpen in Flanders was granted denization in Ireland on 10 April 1605. [IPR]

DE HULTER and Van Homrigh, merchants in Amsterdam, trading with Belfast in 1680. [LHL.Macartney.2] [BMF.181]

DE LA BOUCHETERIE, MARGARET, born 1696 in Ghent, Flanders, daughter of Charles de la Boucheterie, a Colonel on the Irish Establishment, died in Cuffe Street, Dublin, in 1788. [SM.50.51]

DE LA CROYSE, HENRY a merchant from Dunkirk who settled in Wexford around 1640, sent a cargo of pipe staves aboard the Adventure, master Paul Dodd bound for San Lucar in Spain in 1643. [NA.HCA.30.863.1159]

DE LA HEYT, OLIVER, from Dublin, married Machteltje Jans from Rotterdam in the Reformed Church in Rotterdam on 21 January 1698.

DE LARD, PETER, a Fleming residing in Waterford, entered the service, at Dunkirk, Flanders, of Captain Clement Van De Ryder master of the privateer Cornelius of Wexford in October 1649. [TNA.HCA.13.250]

DE LAUN, CHARLES, son of Gideon De Laun and his wife Abigail in Ship Street, Dublin, was baptised in St Bride's on 15 March 1711.

DE LAUN, WILLIAM, son of Gideon De Laun and his wife Abigail in Ship Street, Dublin, was baptised in St Bride's on 8 March 1710.

DE LEON, ABRAHAM, from Endovan in Brabant, was naturalised in Ireland on 12 October 1621. [IPR]

DE MILLY, PAUL, a gentleman from Den Haag in Holland, was denizised in Ireland on 13 April 1670. [IPR]

DEMPSEY, CURA, a Captain of Colonel James Dempsey's Irish Regiment in the Low Countries from 1660 until 1662. [WG]

DEMPSEY, DANIEL, a Captain of Colonel John Morphy's Irish Regiment in Flanders from 1646 until 1659; a Captain of Taafe's Irish Regiment in the Low Countries from 1672 to 1673; Major of Taafe's Irish Regiment in the Low Countries from 1672 until 1673; Major of Colonel Denis O'Byrne's Irish Regiment in the Low Countries from 1673 until 1686. [WG]

DEMPSEY, DENIS, a Captain of Colonel James Dempsey's Irish Regiment in the Low Countries from 1660 until 1662. [WG]

DEMPSEY, DERMOT, a Captain of Colonel John Morphy's Irish Regiment in Flanders from 1646 until 1659. [WG]

DEMPSEY, JAMES, Colonel of an Irish Regiment in the Low Countries from 1660 to 1662. [WG]

DEMPSEY, JAMES, a Captain of Colonel James Dempsey's Irish Regiment in the Low Countries from 1660 until 1662. [WG]

DEMPSEY, MARIRUT, an Ensign of Colonel John Morphy's Irish Regiment in Flanders from 1646 until 1659. [WG]

DEMPSEY, PETER, a chaplain of Colonel James Dempsey's Irish Regiment in the Low Countries from 1660 until 1662. [WG]

DEMPSTER, ROGER, a Captain of Colonel James Dempsey's Irish Regiment in the Low Countries from 1660 until 1662. [WG]

DENNIS, MICHAEL, a merchant from Ypperin [Ypres] in Flanders, was denized in Ireland on 16 January 1671. [IPR]

DENNIS, ROBERT, from Londonderry, married Mary Gambel from London, in the Presbyterian Church in Rotterdam on 25 June 1719.[RA]

DENNY, ARTHUR, from Cork, an army sergeant who died overseas, probate 1693 Prerogative Court of Canterbury, [TNA]

DE NEEF, ANSTANCE, in Cellarstown Shee, County Kilkenny, probate 1765, Diocese of Kilkenny

DE RAET, JANE GERTRUDE, refence to in will of Abel De Le Deveze, probate 1749, Prerogative Court of Canterbury. [TNA]

DE WITT, CLAUS, the cook aboard the Bloem van Amsterdam [Flora of Amsterdam], at the port of Ventry in County Kerry, later captured by the Mermaid an English privateer. [TNA.HCA13.248]

DE WITT, JAN, on board the Bloem van Amsterdam [Flora of Amsterdam], at the port of Ventry in County Kerry, later captured by the Mermaid an English privateer. [TNA.HCA13.248]

DER ANTE, PETER, a surgeon in Waterford, a will dated 1769.

DERRICKSON, JACOB, born 1613, from Wander in Holland, master of the Sant Jacob van Middelburg, [St James of Middelburg], was bound from Waterford to Middelburg in Zealand was examined before the High Court of the Admiralty of England in 1649. [TNA.HCA.13.61]; master Jacob Derrickson of the Sant Jacob van Rotterdam [St James of Rotterdam], was captured by Richard Willoughby, master of the Nonsuch when bound from Waterford in Ireland to Middelburg in Zealand in 1649. [TNA.HCA.13/61.290]

DE RUTER, ANDREAS, in Danzig, [Gdansk] a letter to Daniel Missenden in Belfast on 4 October 1755. [PRONI.D354.775]

DE YONGHE, WILLIAM, a student at Louvain University in 1617. [RCPE]

DES HAES, GABRIEL, from Antwerpen, Flanders, was denizised in Ireland on 10 April 1605. [IPR]

DE SCHOODT, ALEXANDER, a merchant in Antwerpen freighted the St Francis van Antwerpen to sail from Antwerpen to Dublin and to Scotland but was shipwrecked in 1666. [NRS.RH9.5.31]

DESMOND, CORNELIUS, preacher of Henry O'Neill's Irish Regiment in Flanders in 1605. [WG]

DES MYNIERES, LEWIS, from Amersfoot, Utrecht, was denizised in Ireland on 11 December 1655. [IPR]; a merchant in Ireland, who petitioned King Charles II about trade with the Canary Islands in August 1666. [CSPIre]

DEVENISH, Marquis of, born 1670 in Ireland, a Major General in the Emperor's service, was the Governor of Kortrijk in Flanders, died 1740 in Brussels. [SM.2.237]

DE WITT, CLAUS, cook aboard the Bloem van Amsterdam [Flora of Amsterdam], at the port of Ventry in County Kerry, later captured by the Mermaid an English privateer. [TNA.HCA13.248]

DIEKS, O'BRIAN, born 1698, an Irish student at Leiden University in 1720.

DILLON, CHARLES, Colonel, of an Irish Regiment bound for the Low Countries in 1653. [WG]

DILLON, CHRISTOPHER, a Captain of Colonel Charles Dillon's Regiment bound for Flanders in 1653. [WG]

DILLON, GERARD, a Captain of Colonel Charles Dillon's Regiment bound for Flanders in 1653; a Captain of Colonel John Morphy's Irish Regiment in Flanders from 1646 until 1659. [WG]

DILLON, THEOBALD, from Dublin, was admitted as a citizen of Rotterdam on 15 July 1747; married Susanna Edwards from Rotterdam, in the City Church in Rotterdam on 15 March 1752. [RA]

DIN, ARTHUR, from Ireland, married Lena Morris from Rotterdam, in the Presbyterian Church there on 23 August 1722. [RA]

DIXON, JAMES, a Sergeant of Colonel John Morphy's Irish Regiment in Flanders from 1646 until 1659. [WG]

DOBBIN, JAMES, an Irish student at the University of Utrecht in 1720. [UU]

DOLART, THOMAS, a Captain of Colonel Theodore O'Meara's Irish Regiment in the Low Countries from 1660 to 1664. [WG]

DONGAN, THOMAS, born 1634 in County Kildare, an officer of the French Army Colonel of an Irish Regiment in French Service, moved to England where King Charles II appointed him as Major General of the Army in Flanders, Governor of New York from 1682 until 1688, died in London in 1715.

DONNELLY, HENRY, a Captain of Colonel George Cusack's Regiment in the Low Countries from 1656 until 1662. [WG]

DORAN, Captain, master of the St Francis, captured a ship bound from Amsterdam to Dublin and Carrickfergus in May 1644. [TNA.HCA13/58.631]

DORIOVAN, Dr MORGAN, born 1707, an Irish student at Leiden University in 1731.[LU]

DOWLIN, PATRICK, born in Ireland, master of a privateer in American service, based at Duinkeken, [Dunkirk] during the American Revolutionary War, [MHS]

DOWNE, Lord Viscount, died at the Battle of Campen in 1760. [SM.22.669]

DOYLE, WILLIAM, from Waterford, was admitted as a citizen of Rotterdam on 9 November 1726. [RA]

DOYNE, JAMES, master of the Thomas from Ireland with a cargo of beef, pork, butter, tallow, salmon, and feathers bound for Mathew Everard, an Irish merchant, in Dunkirk was shipwrecked near the Isle of Wight on 21 January 1655. [TNA.HCA.13.70.462]. Walter Devereux, born 1625, a merchant in Waterford, survived the shipwreck.

DRAKE, PETER, was among the soldiers who left Ireland after the Treaty of Limerick in October 1691, he enrolled in Colonel Athur Dillon's Regiment of Foot, and fought for France against the British at Ramillies and at Malplaquet in 1709, in 1707 he served aboard Dunkirk privateer attacking British ships, he moved to London where he was pardoned then joined Marlborough's Army and was stationed at Ghent.

DREW, BARNEY, born in 1717, an Irish student at the University of Leiden in 1740. [UL]

DREW, EDWARD, a Lieutenant of the 27th [Inniskilling] Regiment, was wounded at the Battle of Waterloo in 1815.

DREW, FRANCIS, an Irish academic at the University of Leiden in 1744. [UL]

DRISCOLL, CORNELIUS, Captain of Colonel Henry O'Neill's Irish Regiment in Flanders in 1605. [WG]

DRISCOLL, MACON, Sergeant of Colonel Henry O'Neill's Irish Regiment in Flander in 1605. [WG]

DRUM, JAMES, Sergeant of Colonel Henry O'Neill's Irish Regiment in Flanders in 1605. [WG]

DUDAL, FRANCIS, a Captain of Colonel John Morphy's Irish Regiment in Flanders from 1646 until 1659. [WG]

DUDAL, HENRY, an Ensign of Colonel Dermot O'Sullivan's Irish Regiment in Flanders, from 1646 until 1647. [WG]

DUFF, THOMAS, an Irish merchant loaded a cargo including tobacco aboard the Rowland of Bremen at Emden in March 1643 bound for Wexford but was shipwrecked off the coast of Wales. [TNA.HCA.13.58]

DUGGAN, CHARLES, born 1680, an Irish student at Leiden University in 1700. [AH.59][UL]

DUIET, PATRICK, an Ensign of Colonel Denis O'Byrne's Irish Regiment in the Low Countries from 1673 until 1686

DULONGE, JEAN, and SONS, in Amsterdam, reference to in a letter dated 24 July 1755. [PRONI.D353.765]

DUNCAN, JOHN, a soldier from Ireland, married Anne Thomson, from Scotland, widow of William Livingston, in Leide, Holland, on 11 July 1603. [Leiden Marriage Register]

DUNGAN, CHRISTOPHER, a Captain of Colonel Thomas Preston's Irish Regiment in Flanders from 1634 until 1641. [WG]

DUNGAN, MARK, a Captain of Colonel Owen Roe O'Neill's Irish Regiment in Flanders from 1633 until 1642. [WG]

DURRHAN, Captain, master of a Dunkirk man-of-war captured the Adventure of London, master Paul Dodd, which was then taken to Wexford in 1648. [TNA.HCA.15.5.885]

DYAT, HUGH, master of the Hanover from Belfast to Rotterdam on 21 March 1738. [PRONI.D354.518]

DYER, DENIS, a Captain of Colonel Thomas Preston's Irish Regiment in Flanders from 1634 until 1641. [WG]

EEDBETTEL, JOSEPH, born 1705, an Irish Student at the University of Leiden in 1733. [UL]

EDWARDS, ETON, born 1694, an Irish student at Leiden University in 1714.[UL]

EDWARD, JOHN, from Swigdale, Ireland, married Cathrin Jameson, from 'Heratogenbosch, in the City Church in Rotterdam on 3 June 1650. [RA]

EDWARDS, MARTIN, born in 1722, an Irish student at the University of Leiden in 1742. [UL]

EDWARDS, MICHAEL, from Dublin, was admitted as a citizen of Rotterdam on 8 June 1728. [RA]

EDWARDS, THOMAS, from Dublin, was admitted as a citizen of Rotterdam on 22 April 1747. [RA]

EGAN, EWAN, a Chaplain of Colonel George Cusack's Regiment in the Low Countries from 1656 until 1662. [WG]

EGAN, SOLOMAN, an Ensign of Colonel Denis O'Byrne's Irish Regiment in the Low Countries from 1673 until 1686. [WG]

ELFORT, STEPHEN, the Chief Surgeon of Colonel Patrick Fitzgerald's Regiment in Flanders from 1639 until 1641. [WG]

EMKEN, ABRAHAM, a merchant from Amsterdam was naturalised in Ireland on 7 November 1662. [BL.Egerton.77][IPR]

ENGELS, JOHANN, from Dublin, was admitted as a citizen of Rotterdam on 29 April 1763. [RA]

ERRINGTON, EDWARD, an Ensign of MacElligott's Regiment in Flanders in 1688. [IS]

ERWYN, GERHARD, an Irish student at the University of Leiden in 1728. [UL]

EUSTACE, EDWARD, Captain of Colonel Thomas Preston's Irish Regiment in Flanders from 1634 until 1641. [WG]

EUSTACE, Captain OLIVER, a soldier in Flanders, plotted with Stephen de Ibarra the Spanish secretary of the Council of War in Flanders around 1590. [DPR.299]

EVERSON, SYMON, from Utrecht, resident of Cork, was naturalised in Ireland in September 1663. [BL.Egerton.77] [IPR]

FA, THADEUS, Sergeant of Colonel Henry O'Neill's Irish Regiment in Flanders in 1605. [WG]

FALLAN, LAWRENCE, Captain of Colonel William Stanley's Irish Regiment, sent to support the Dutch against the Spanish from 1586 until 1587 when the regiment changed allegiance in favour of Spain until 1604. [WG]

FALVY, ALEXIS, a Chaplain of the Earl of Bristol's Irish Regiment bound for the Low Countries in 1657. [G]

FANNING, JAMES, born 1615, a merchant of Limerick, trading in Holland and Zealand in 1648. [TNA.HCA.13.249]

FANNING, RICHARD, a Captain of Colonel Dermot O'Sullivan's Irish Regiment in Flanders from 1646 until 1647; a Captain of Colonel John Morphy's Irish Regiment in Flanders from 1646 until 1659. [WG]

FARNELL, JOHN, born 1710, an Irish Student at the University of Leiden in 1735. [UL]

FARELL, CONNELL, Lieutenant Colonel of [formerly the Earl of Bristol's] Colonel Louis Farrell's Irish Regiment] bound for the Low Countries in 1658 to 1660 [WG]

FARRELL, DERMOT, a Sergeant of Colonel John Morphy's Irish Regiment in Flanders from 1646 until 1659. [WG]

FARRELL, EDMUND, born 1717, an Irish student at the University of Leiden in 1745; from Dublin, married Barbara Swennen, in the City Church of Rotterdam on 12 June 1746. [UL][RA]

FARRELL, JAMES, Major of Colonel Louis Farrell's [formerly the Earl of Bristol's] Irish Regiment] bound for the Low Countries in 1658-1660 [WG]

FARRELL, LOUIS, Colonel of [formerly the Earl of Bristol's] an Irish Regiment bound for the Low Countries in 1658-1660 [WG]

FARRELL, THADEUS, an Ensign of Colonel John Morphy's Irish Regiment in Flanders from 1646 until 1659. [WG]

FEARNES, ANTONY, born in 1703, an Irish student at the University of Leiden in 1726. [UL]

FENIX, PIETER, from Ireland, married Elisabeth Miels from Norfolk, in the Reformed Church of Rotterdam on 8 April 1691. [RA]

FERAL, Licentiate WILLIAM, chaplain of Captain Thadeus Souliman's Company in the Earl of Tyrone's Regiment, a licence to return to Ireland on account of his father's death there, dated Brussels, 4 April 1630. [AGRB]

FERGUSON, JOHN, born 1699, an Anglo-Irish student at Leiden University in 1719. [UL]

FERGUSON, JOHN, born 1697, an Irish student at Leiden University in 1720.[UL]

FERRIER, HENRY, a Captain of Colonel Theodore O'Meara's Irish Regiment in the Low Countries from 1660 to 1664. [WG]

FERRITER, RICHARD, a Captain of Colonel Theodore O'Meara's Irish Regiment in the Low Countries from 1660 to 1664. [WG]

FINGLAS, THOMAS, persuaded Irish soldiers to defect from the Army of Flanders to the Service of the States General around 1587.

FITCHYMERS, DANIEL, born 1689, an Irish student at Leiden University in 1714.[UL]

FITZGERALD, Lord EDWARD, married Pamela, daughter of the Duke of Orleans in Doornik [Tournai] Flanders in 1792. [SM.55.49]

FITZGERALD, GEORGE, Captain of MacElligott's Regiment in Flanders around 1688. [IS]

FITZGERALD, GERALD, of Colonel Stanley's Regiment at Spa in 1589. [AGRB.16]

FITZGERALD, Major GERALD, served abroad as Captain and later Major of Colonel John Fitzgerald's Regiment, under the Duke of Ormonde, petitioned King Charles II for the restoration of lands in County Limerick, in 1669. [SPIre]

FITZGERALD, PATRICK, was in the Low Countries by 1631, Colonel of an Irish Regiment in Flanders from 1639 to 1641, when it was ordered to embark for Spain. [WG]

FITZGERALD, THOMAS, a Captain of Colonel John Morphy's Irish Regiment in Flanders from 1646 until 1659. [WG]

FITZHERBERT, ANDREW, born 1712, an Irish Student at the University of Leiden in 1737. [UL]

FITZPATRICK, ANDREW, born 1710, an Irish Student at the University of Leiden in 1736. [UL]

FITZPATRICK, JOSEPH, born 1710, an Irish Student at the University of Leiden from 1736 until 1739. [UL]

FITZSIMON, DANIEL, born 1686, an Irish student at Leiden University in 1716. [UL]

FLAHARTY, MORGAN, a Captain of Colonel George Cusack's Regiment in the Low Countries from 1656 until 1662. [WG]

FLEMING, JOHN, an Irish soldier in Tournai, Flanders, in 1582. [AGRB.1]

FLEMING, JOHN, a Captain of Colonel Owen Roe O'Neill's Irish Regiment in Flanders from 1633 until 1642. [WG]

FLEMING, JOHN, from Dublin, married Aagje Jacobs, the widow of Jacob Antonis, from Rotterdam, in the Reformed Church there on 24 November 1733. [RA]

FLEMING, ROBERT, a Captain of Colonel Hugh O'Donnell's Regiment in Flanders from 1632 until 1638. [WG]

FLINN, BALACK, a Captain of Colonel Charles Dillon's Regiment bound for Flanders in 1653; a Captain of Colonel John Morphy's Irish Regiment in Flanders from 1646 until 1659. [WG]

FLINN, DONALD, an Ensign of Colonel John Morphy's Irish Regiment in Flanders from 1646 until 1659. [WG]

FLINN, THOMAS, an Ensign of Colonel John Morphy's Irish Regiment in Flanders from 1646 until 1659. [WG]

FOLEY, WALTER, born in 1712, an Irish student at the University of Leiden in 1737. [UL]

FOULT, JERIMIAS, from Dublin, married Maria de la Hais from Rotterdam, in the Reformed Church there on 22 July 1612.

FOWKE, JOHN, born 1703 an Irish student at Leiden University in 1725. [UL]

FOX, THOMAS, an Ensign of Colonel James Dempsey's Irish Regiment in the Low Countries from 1660 until 1662. [WG]

FRANCIS, OLIVER, born in Flanders, captain of the St Michael the Archangel, was, around 1642, granted Letters of Marque authorising him to be a privateer at sea attacking the enemies of Catholicism in Ireland and opponents of King Charles I. [MM.76.121]

FRANKLAND, RICHARD, born in 1702, an Irish student at the University of Leiden in 1725, an Irish academic at the University of Leiden in 1728. [UL]

FREEMAN, HENRY, born 1713 an Irish student at the University of Leiden in 1733.[UL]

FRENCH, ANTHONY, Judge Advocate of Colonel George Cusack's Regiment in the Low Countries from 1656 until 1662. [WG]

FRENCH, ROBERT, born 1696, an Irish student at Leiden University in 1718. [UL]

FRENCH, WILLIAM, [Williem Frens], from Westport in Ireland, a pirate in 1614. [PPN.App.vi]

FRIMAN, MATTHEW, from Limerick, was admitted as a citizen of Rotterdam on 10 November 1793.[RA]

GAFRY, DENIS, a Chaplain to Captain Malachy O'Morra's Company of the Earl of Tyrconnel's Regiment in 1632. [AGRB.1221]

GAMELSEN, SVENSE, master of the Angel Gabriel of Copenhagen contracted in Amsterdam, with   James Fanning, born 1615, and Marcus Rich, born 1618, merchants from Limerick, to take a cargo of iron, tobacco, wine, deals, indigo, figs, raisins, olives, capers, currants hops, madder, etc to their factor at Limerick or Galway, however the vessel was attacked and sunk off the coast of Cornwall on 3 February 1648 by Captain Thomas Bedell of the Adventure.   [TNA.HCA.13.249.616]

GARDINER, BARTHOLOMEW, of Colonel Stanley's Regiment at Spa in 1589. [AGRB.16]

GARLAND, JAMES, Ensign of Colonel Henry O'Neill's Irish Regiment in Flanders in 1605. [WG]

GARLAND, Captain, a soldier in Dutch service around 1757, reference. [PRONI.D354.995]

GARLON, PATRICK, a Captain of Colonel Patrick O'Donnell's Irish Regiment in Flanders from 1643 to 1647. [WG]

GARSTIN, JOHN, born 1691, an Irish student at the University of Leiden in 1713. [UL]

GARVIE, LUKE, a Chaplain of Colonel George Cusack's Regiment in the Low Countries from 1656 until 1662. [WG]

GEAGIN, MALACHY, an Ensign of Colonel James Dempsey's Irish Regiment in the Low Countries from 1660 until 1662. [WG]

GEOGHAGEN, FRANCIS, Quartermaster of Taafe's Irish Regiment in the Low Countries from 1672 until 1673. [WG]

GEFFREY, JAMES, Captain of Colonel Patrick Fitzgerald's Regiment in Flanders from 1639 until 1641. [WG]

GEFFREY, LAWRENCE, a Captain of Colonel Hugh O'Donnell's Regiment in Flanders from 1632 until 1638. [WG]

GERALDIN, CHRISTOPHER, an Ensign of Colonel John Morphy's Irish Regiment in Flanders from 1646 until 1659. [WG]

GERALDIN, EDWARD, a Major of Colonel John O'Neill's Regiment in Flanders from 1610 until 1628. [WG]

GERALDIN, GASPAR, an Irish infantryman in Captain Maurice Geraldin's Company, was granted a commission as Ensign of the said Company, dated Brussels on 10 April 1630. [OGRB]

GERALDIN, JAMES, a Sergeant of Colonel Patrick O'Donnell's Irish Regiment in Flanders from 1643 to 1647. [WG]

GERALDIN, JOHN, a Captain of Colonel Owen Roe O'Neill's Irish Regiment in Flanders from 1633 until 1642. [WG]

GERALDIN, JOHN, an Ensign of Colonel John O'Neill's Regiment in Flanders, 1610-1628. [WG]

GERALDIN, JOHN, Major of Colonel Patrick Fitzgerald in Flanders from 1639 until 1641. [WG]

GERALDIN, OLIVER, of the Irish infantry, to be granted six crowns monthly, Brussels, 1 July 1631. [AGRB]

GERALDIN, PATRICK, a soldier of the Irish infantry, a grant of four crowns monthly by King Philip IV of Spain, dated Brussels 4 July 1631. [AGRB]

GERALDIN, PATRICK, a Captain of Colonel Owen Roe O'Neill's Irish Regiment in Flanders from 1633 until 1642. [WG]

GERALDIN, P., Major of Colonel John Morphy's Irish Regiment in Flanders from 1646 until 1659. [WG]

GERALDIN, PETER, a Captain of Colonel James Dempsey's Irish Regiment in the Low Countries from 1660 until 1662. [WG]

GERALDIN, RICHARD, an Ensign of Colonel John O'Neill's Regiment in Flanders, 1610-1628; a Major of Colonel Thomas Preston's Irish Regiment in Flanders from 1634 until 1641. [WG]

GERALDIN, RAYMOND, was commissioned as a Captain of Irish Infantry to recruit 200 men in 1633. [AGRB.1232]

GERALDIN, THOMAS, a Captain of Colonel Theodore O'Meara's Irish Regiment in the Low Countries from 1660 to 1664. [WG]

GERRITS, ..., from Limerick, married Grietge Davids from Rotterdam in the Reformed Church in Rotterdam on 12 April 1718.

GEYLENSON, MEYLES, from Zealand, a resident of Dublin, was denizised in Ireland on 29 December 1622. [IPR]

GIBBS, JOHN, born 1698, an Irish student at Leiden University in 1720. [UL]

GIBBONS, JOHN, master of the Mary of London from Dublin with a cargo of butter, tallow, and hides bound for Le Havre, was captured by a privateer of Ostend in May 1668 and was taken to Ostend. [SP.Ire.1668.612/6]

GIBSON, ARCHIBALD, in Danzig, a charter party in Dutch with Martin Haubus, dated 12 August 1755. [PRONI.D354.404]

GIFFORD, RICHARD, born 1701, an Irish student at Leiden University in 1722, an Irish academic at the University of Leiden in 1726. [UL]

GIL, ABRAHAM, from Dublin, married Margaretha Vrijoag, from Rotterdam, in the City Church there on 28 October 1736. [RA]

GILBURNE, THOMAS, born 1639, a soldier during Queen Anne's wars, fought under the Duke of Marlborough, including the Battle of Dettingen in 1743 [SM.49.623]

GILL, ISAAC, a merchant from Vlissigen, [Flushing], in Zealand, was denizized in Ireland on 18 July 1666. [IPR]

GILL, JAN, from Londonderry, married Chris Van Coeverden, from Rotterdam in the Reformed Church there on 3 March 1736. [RA]

GILES, PATRICK, Captain of an Irish Regiment, sent to support the Dutch against the Spanish from 1586 until 1587 when the regiment changed allegiance in favour of Spain until 1604. [WG]

GILMAN, GEORGE, a Major of the 27th [Inniskilling] Regiment in Flanders from 1793 until 1795.

37

GODDARD, JOHN, from Cork, was admitted as a citizen of Rotterdam on 14 June 1715. [RA]

GOLDEN, STEPHEN, a chaplain to the Company of Captain Daniel Daly of the Irish Infantry in Flanders in 1631. [AGRB]

GOODMAN, THOMAS, an Ensign of Colonel John O'Neill's Regiment in Flanders, from 1610 until 1628. [WG]

GOR, JAN, from Ireland, married Geertruyd Roos from Rotterdam, in the Reformed Church there on 19 November 1748. [RA]

GORMLEY, BERNARD, senior chaplain of Colonel John O'Neill's Regiment in Flanders from 1610 until 1628. [WG]

GOTT, JAMES, born 1622, from Waterford, Lieutenant of the Mary of Antrim, a Confederate privateer, 120 tons, which was captured by the Tiger on 3 February 1649. [TNA.HCA.13.250]

GOUGH, WILLIAM, from Cork, was admitted as a citizen of Rotterdam on 23 April 1710. [RA]

GRAHAM, JAMES, born 1678, an Irish student at Leiden University in1700. [AH.59][UL]

GRAHAM, RICHARD, from County Down, was admitted as a citizen of Rotterdam on 10 October 1734. [RA]

GRANYER, JAMES, from the Netherlands, was denizised in Ireland on 1 December 1619. [IPR]

GREEN, WILLIAM, born in 1704, an Irish student at the University of Leiden in 1728. [UL]

GRENON, DERBY, Ensign of Colonel Henry O'Neill's Irish Regiment in Flanders in 1605. [WG]

GRIFFIN, SIMON, from Cork, married Margaretha Ophreys from Velo, the Netherlands, in the Reformed Church in Rotterdam on 13 March 1736. [RA]

GRIFFITH, JOHN, from Dublin, married Maria De Rycke in the Reformed Church in Rotterdam on 10 April 1667. [RA]

38

GRIGGE, THOMAS, master of the Discovery captured the St Charles in May 1646 when bound from Dunkerque [Dunkirk] to Limerick. [TNA.HCA]

GROGHEGA, JAMES, a Captain of Colonel George Cusack's Regiment in the Low Countries from 1656 until 1662. [WG]

GROSSET, GREGORY, from Inniskilling, County Fermanagh, married Elizabeth Atkinson in the Presbyterian Church in Rotterdam on 14 June 1711. [RA]

GUNNES, ARTHUR, was born in England, was a seaman aboard the Angel Keeper of Waterford, a Confederate privateer, stated that the crew was mostly from Dunkirk or Flanders at his trial on 21 March 1648. [TNA.HCA.15.2]

GYLBERTSEN, WALTER, a mariner from Howsduyn in Holland, was denisized in Ireland on 5 August 1675. [IPR]

HACKETT, THEOBALD, an Ensign of MacElligott's Regiment in Flanders in 1688. [IS]

HAGAN, HENRY, Captain of Colonel Henry O'Neill's Irish Regiment in Flanders in 1605. [WG]

HALIDENS, SAMUEL, an Irish student at Leiden University in 1705. [UL]

HALL, WILLIAM, a soldier in the King's service in Dunkirk, Flanders, a petition in February 1666. [SPIre]

HALLIDAY, ROBERT DALWAY, born in 1723, an Irish student at the University of Leiden in 1743. [UL]

HALY, EDMUND, a Sergeant of Colonel Dermot O'Sullivan's Irish Regiment in Flanders, from 1646 until 1647. [WG]

HALY, JACOB, and his brother MICHAEL HALY, merchants in Limerick, owners of the Elizabeth of Limerick which they let to George Rochford and Peres Maroney, to ship goods from Limerick to Dunkirk but the vessel was arrested at Falmouth in England in 1642. [TNA.HCA.13.117.468]

HAMILTON, ARCHIBALD, from Belfast, was admitted a citizen of Rotterdam on 20 October 1720; a letter to J. McClure and Company, dated 7 December 1725. [PRONI.D654.B2.35]; in Rotterdam he chartered the Hanover, master Hugh Dyat on 17 February 1739. [PRONI.D354.519]

HAMILTON, ARCHIBALD, from Dublin, married Magdalena Campbell from Rotterdam, in the Reformed Church in Rotterdam on 18 February 1755. [RA]

HAMILTON, EZECHIEL, born 1699, an Irish student at the University of Leiden in 1747. [UL]

HAMILTON, JAMES, born in 1704, an Irish student at the University of Leiden in 1725. [UL]

HAMILTON, JAMES, born 1729, an Irish student at the University of Leiden in 1749. [UL]

HAMILTON, LESLIE, born in 1713, an Irish student at the University of Leiden in 1743. [UL]

HAMILTON, SAMPSON, born in 1718, an Irish student at the University of Leiden in 1738. [UL]

HANDSHILL, HENRY, master of the City of Hamburg with a cargo belonging to Philip Van Porten, a merchant in Hamburg, when bound for Archangel, Russia, was captured by Henry Martin, master of the Charlotte of Calais in 1674. [NRS.HCAS.AC7.5]

HARE, JOHN, Major of the 27th [Enniskillen] Regiment at the Battle of Waterloo in 1815.

HARLING, RANDALL, captured the Jan van Duinkerken in July 1644 when bound from Duinkerken [Dunkirk] to Waterford. [TNA.HCA.13/246]

HARMANS, JOHN, an Irish soldier and a vagrant, who was banished from Leiden, in Holland, on 11 January 1641. [PL.111]

HARPERT, JOHN, from Ireland, was admitted as a citizen of Rotterdam on 6 September 1738. [RA]

HARPER THOMAS, from Wexford, was admitted as a citizen of Rotterdam on 19 December 1709. [RA]

HARRIN, JOHN, an Irish doctor in the Regiment of Colonel Stanley in 1590. [AGRB.32]

HARRIS, JOHN, from Ireland, married Heyndrickje Jans from Rotterdam, in the Reformed Church in Rotterdam on 23 February 1676.

HARRISON, WALTER, a Captain of Colonel Dermot O'Sullivan's Irish Regiment in Flanders, from 1646 until 1647; a Captain of Colonel John Morphy's Irish Regiment in Flanders from 1646 until 1659. [WG]

HARVEY, JOHN, born 1710, an Irish student at the University of Leiden in 1731. [UL]

HARVEY, THOMAS, jr., an Englishman residing in Ireland, aboard the Golden Lion bound from Rotterdam for the East Indies, a testament dated 17 March 1621. [ONA.Rotterdam.102/115/168]

HAYES, WALTER, master of the Patrick of Waterford when bound from Duinkerken [Dunkirk] to Dublin, was captured and taken to Dartmouth, England, in January 1642. [TNA.HCA13.58.18].

HEESTER, JAMES, a merchant, from Holland, was naturalised in Ireland on 27 January 1662. [BL.ms.Egerton.77]

HEINSSEN, JORIS, from Flanders, a master gunner's mate aboard a privateer in 1614. . [PPN.Appx.vi]

HEMPHILL, JAMES, from Ballymoney, was admitted as a citizen of Rotterdam on 21 January 1727. [RA]

HEMSWORTH, JOHN, born 1705, an Irish student at Leiden University in 1725. [UL]

HENDERS, DERRICK, late of Dunkirk, Flanders, master of the St John of Waterford, 25 July 1649. [TNA.HCA.13.250]

HENDERSON, JAN, from Dublin, married Anna Paartz from Dublin, in the Reformed Church of Rotterdam in 1660. [RA]

HENDES, DERRICK, from Duinkerken [Dunkirk], master of the St John of Waterford was tried as a privateer on 25 July 1649. [TNA.HCA.13.250]

HENDRICKS, Father PIETER, a Dutch Carmelite, was sent to Ireland in 1642, settled in Waterford, a petition to remain in Ireland, dated 1651. [TNA.HCA.13.252]

HENERY, D., P., in Utrecht, a letter to L. Percival, dated 15 July 1702. [PRONI.D906.61]

HENSON, FLORENCE, born 1722, an Irish student at the University of Leiden in 1748, an Irish academic at the University of Leiden in 1749. [UL]

HERNAN, JAMES, a Captain of Colonel John Morphy's Irish Regiment in Flanders from 1646 until 1659. [WG]

HERNE, JAMES, born 1683, from Dublin, an Irish student at Leiden University in 1705. [AH.59][UL]

HERPERTS, PATRICK, from Ireland married Adriana Kerckman from Rotterdam, in the City Church in Rotterdam on 2 November 1692. [RA]

HEWETSON, PATRICK, born in 1702, an Irish student at the University of Leiden.   [UL]

HEY, DAVID, a Sergeant of Colonel George Cusack's Regiment in the Low Countries from 1656 until 1662. [WG]

HEYDEN, GEORGE, a Captain of Colonel James Dempsey's Irish Regiment in the Low Countries from 1660 until 1662. [WG]

HIERLEY, CORNELIS, from Ireland, married Anna Wade, widow of John Cullen, from Ireland in the City Church in Rotterdam on 27 April 1760. [RA]

HILANGHT, THOMAS, from Cork, married Jannetgen Jans from Dysart, [Scotland?] in the Reformed Church in Rotterdam on 21 March 1649. [RA]

HILL, ROBERT, the Dutch Consul in Cork, referred to in the Will of Jonathan Perrie in Cork dated 30 May 1709 in Dublin.

HILL, ..., an Ensign of MacElligott's Regiment in Flanders in 1688. [IS]

HINDERSON, NICHOLAS, born 1616, master's mate of the Rosecrane of Amsterdam with 180 Irish soldiers bound from Galway for Vlissingen [Flushing] in 1649 but was captured by a Parliamentary frigate, the Tiger's Whelp, and taken to Milford Haven in Wales in April 1649. [TNA.HCA.13.250]

HOGAN, PATRICK, born 1793 in Killarney, County Kerry, enlisted in the British Army on 9 May 1812, a Sergeant of the 73rd Regiment of Foot, lost an arm at the Battle of Waterloo in 1815, was discharged on 24 October 1816, died in 1863. [TNA.WO2/73/103]

HOLLAND, CORNELIUS, a landowner at Great Ardrums, County Meath, in 1667. [SPIre]

HOLT, JOHN PETERS VTEN, a commissary was sent by the States of the Netherlands to Kinsale, County Cork, to negotiate the liberty of The Red Lion of Amsterdam and other Dutch ships detained in Ireland in 1649. [TNA.HCA.13.250]

HOPE, GERALD, a Captain of Colonel Hugh O'Donnell's Regiment in Flanders from 1632 until 1638. [WG]

HOPE, WALTER, Captain of the Duke of Gloucester's Regiment fought in Flanders, son of Alexander Hope of Molingar, petitioned King Charles II in June 1661. [CSPIre]

HOPE, Sergeant, of the Earl of Tyrone's Irish infantry was sent to Ireland to recruit a company of infantry in 1632. [AGRB.1187]

HOPPER, ANTHONY, born 1664, fought under King William at the Battle of the Boyne, later served under the Duke of Marlborough in Germany, died in Cork on 11 September 1779. [SM.41.511]

HORNE, WILLIAM, master of the Mary Consolation of Waterford was captured at sea in August 1647 by Captain Gilson of the Constant Warwick. [TNA.HCA.13.60]

HOUSTOUN, ROBERT, born in 1714, an Irish student at the University of Leiden in 1740. [UL]

HOUSTOUN, WILLIAM, an Ensign of Colonel John Morphy's Irish Regiment in Flanders from 1646 until 1659. [WG]

HOVILLE, WILLIAM, born 1620, from Waterford, master of the privateer Angel Keeper of Waterford around 1648, some of his captures were taken to Ostend. [TNA.HCA.13.58.820]

HOWERS, CORNELIUS, master of the Flora of Amsterdam from St Michael's in the Western Islands, with a cargo bound for Amsterdam was captured by the Mermaid, Captain Williams, a Parliamentary warship, and took it to Kinsale. The crew of the Flora included Claes De Witt the cook, born 1621; Lambert Lubert the steersman, born 1591; John De Witt the gunner, born 1625; and Jacob Johnson, the carpenter, born 1617; and Charles Anderson. An inventory of the cargo of the Flora was taken by William Broadbeere, Hugh Percival, Willim Hovill, and Strangeman Mendham, merchants in Kinsale. [TNA.HCA.13.248.569]

HOY, PHILIP, a Captain of Colonel George Cusack's Regiment in the Low Countries from 1656 until 1662. [WG]

HUGH, ALEXANDER, from Tilibol parish in Cork, married Mary Horn, daughter of William Horn, from Culross, Scotland, in the Scots Kirk in Rotterdam, on 22 June 1707. [RA]

HUGH, JOHN M, born 1703, an Irish student at the University of Leiden in 1729. [UL]

HULLACAN, DERMOT, chaplain of an Colonel Henry O'Neill's Irish Regiment in Flanders in 1605. [WG]

IRISH, TIERLO MAHONIER, a soldier in Spanish service in Flanders and by 1602 in Spain. [AGS.E.Leg.2764]

ISBRANT, GERRALD, master of The Mary Magdalene of Wexford, a 16 ton frigate, and a privateer during 1640s. [MM.76.123]

IVOIR, MAURICE, a Chief Surgeon of Taafe's Irish Regiment in the Low Countries from 1672 until 1673. [WG]

JACOBS, HERMAN, in Limerick, a letter to Daniel Mussenden in Belfast on 21 December 1756, regarding trade there, and states that Captains Bohde, Steengrove and Beingsman, have sailed with cargoes of butter, but that Captain Wischusen remans in port. [PRONI.D354.669]

JACOBS, ISAAC, in Waterford, a letter to Thomas Greer in Dungannon, County Tyrone, dated 2 January 1781. [PRONI.D1044.628]

JACOBSON, ISBRAND, master of the St Jacob of Rotterdam, later known as the St Jacob of Middelsburg, from Rotterdam with rye bound for Bristol, England, but was captured by the frigate Mary of Antrim a privateer of the Catholic Confederates in October 1648. [TNA.HCA.30.549]

JACOBSON, IVE, born 1609, from Winckle in Holland, master of the Rosecrane of Amsterdam with 180 Irish soldiers bound from Galway for Vlissingen [Flushing] in 1649 but was captured by a Parliamentary frigate, the Tiger's Whelp, and taken to Milford Haven in Wales in April 1649. [TNA.HCA.13.250]

JACOBSON, JACOB, master of the Sant Jan van Rotterdam [St John of Amsterdam], was captured by privateers near Dublin in September 1645.

[TNA.HCA.13.60] also the <u>Rebecca and Roebuck,</u> when bound from St Martins in France to Dublin and Wexford in 1745. [TNA.HCA.13.60]

JANS, EDWARD, in Dublin, a bond dated 1640. [PRONI.D430.145]

JANSSE, JAN, from Ireland, married Christina Davids, widow of Jan Jacobz., in the Reformed Church in Rotterdam on 3 October 1652. [RA]

JANS, MARIA, widow of Francis Taylor in Dublin, a deed dated 1650. [PRONI.D430.155]

JANSEN, REYNIER, from Ireland, married Anna Van Den Plasveld from Antwerpen, Flanders, in the Reformed Church in Rotterdam on 27 March 1588. [RA]

JASPERS, JOHN, from the Netherlands, was denizised in Ireland on 27 February 1635. [IPR]

JEKSON, JORIS, from Rosh in Ireland, married Christina Willems, from Rotterdam, in the Reformed Church there on 20 September 1733. [NB. The bride was already married but had been abandoned by her husband] [RA]

JENISON, JOHN, born 1711, an Irish Student at the University of Leiden in 1731. [UL]

JENNON, JOHN, an Ensign of MacElligott's Regiment in Flanders in 1688. [IS]

JOHNSON, CORNELIUS, from Ossanen in the Netherlands, was denizised in Ireland on 1 December 1619. [IPR]

JOHNSON, GARRET, a merchant who was licensed to export linen yarn from Ireland to the Low Countries on 4 September 1627. [CPRIre.i.237]

JOHNSON, HENRY, master of the <u>Anne van Amsterdam,</u> [Anne of Amsterdam] when bound from Wales to Holland in September 1645, was captured by Richard Willoughby, master of the <u>Globe.</u> [TNA.HCA.13//63.284; HCA.30/495]

GONZALES EMANUEL, from Portugal, master of the galliot <u>St Clara of Waterford,</u> a privateer with a commission by Lord Muskerry to seize all English and Scottish ships, sailed from Waterford on 29 December 1648 but was captured by Anthony Young, master of the <u>Dragon</u> on 3 January

1649. Among the crew were Henry Johnson a mariner from Serdam in Holland, Meevan Dirrickson a mariner from Dunkirk, and Gabriel Perina a mariner from Almada in Portugal. [TNA.HCA.15.5.902]

JOHNSON, JACOB, carpenter aboard the Bloem van Amsterdam [Flora of Amsterdam], at the port of Ventry in County Kerry, later captured by the Mermaid an English privateer. [TNA.HCA13.248]

JOHNSON, LAURENCE, master of the Sint Pieter van Amsterdam [St Peter of Amsterdam] when bound from Oostende [Ostend] to St Sebastian in Spain, was captured by Thomas Plunkett, master of the Discovery in February 1645. [TNA.HCA.]

JOHNSON, MARTIN VON HYNINGE, a Dutch fuller in Lisburn, Ireland in August 1665. [SPIre.1663-1665.617]

JOHNSTON, CATHERINE, from Ireland, married Alexander Melville from Carriden, West Lothian, in the Scots Kirk in Rotterdam on 24 October 1708. [GAR]

JOHNSTON, JAMES, from Dublin, married Geertruyda Adriana Ver Huysen, from Rotterdam, in the City Church of Rotterdam, on 26 July 1700. [RA]

JOHNSTON, JOHN, born 1648, a Scots-Irish student of Philosophy at the University of Leiden in 1669. [AH.59][UL]

JOHNSTON, WILLIAM, a Lieutenant of MacElligott's Regiment around 1688. [IS]

JONASSEN, DIRCK, from Ireland, married Elizabeth Mitchell from England, in the Reformed Church in Rotterdam on 21 October 1635. [RA]

JONES, CONWAY, an Irish academic at the University of Leiden in 1743. [UL]

JORDAN, JOHN, an Ensign of Colonel John O'Neill's Regiment in Flanders, from   1611 to 1628. [WG]

JORDAN, RICHARD, from Dublin, married Annetje Backster from England in the City Church of Rotterdam on 27 September 1663. [RA]

JORISE, ADRIAN, master of the Ann of Rotterdam, from Dublin via Aberdovy in Wales, bound for Rotterdam in June 1645. [TNA.HCA.30.394]

JURIANS, PIETER, a mariner from Cawdon in Friesland, the Netherlands, was denizised in Ireland on 15 June 1671. [IPR]

KEARNAN, WILLIAM, from Ballintober, Ireland, died in Amsterdam, probate 1657, Prerogative Court of Canterbury. [TNA]

KEATING, RICHARD, born 1623, from Ballanycrag in Ireland, a soldier in Flanders, was a witness before the High Court of the Admiralty of England in January 1648. [TNA.HCA.13.62.64]

KEATING, Captain RICHARD, master of the Delight of Cork was granted Letters of Marque on 30 May 1649, he captured the Lead van Vlissingen in September 1649. [TNA.HCA.13.250]

KELLY, DAVID, from Limerick, on board the Elizabeth of Limerick from Limerick bound for Dunkirk in 1642.

KELLY, HUGH, from Dublin, married Maria Cleere from Nantes, France, in Rotterdam City Church on 23 January 1724. [RA]

KELLY, JOHN, an Irish soldier, Ensign of the Light Horse, formerly of the Lancers in 1588. [AGRB.7]

KELLY, JOHN, an Ensign of Colonel John Morphy's Irish Regiment in Flanders from 1646 until 1659. [WG]

KELLY, JOHN, born 1710, an Irish Student at the University of Leiden in 1735. [UL]

KELLY, THOMAS, Sergeant of Colonel Henry O'Neill's Irish Regiment in Flanders in 1605. [WG]

KELLY, THOMAS, from Ireland, was admitted as a citizen of Rotterdam on 6 June 1771. [RA]

KELLY, WILLIAM, a Sergeant of Colonel Hugh O'Donnell's Regiment in Flanders from 1632 until 1638. [WG]

KENNEDY, ANTONY, born 1677, an Irish student at Leiden University in 1697. [AH.59]

KENNEDY, BERNARD, a Captain of Colonel Theodore O'Meara's Irish Regiment in the Low Countries from 1660 to 1664. [WG]

KENNEDY, DANIEL, a privateer with Letters of Marque, active in the East Indies, was captured by the Dutch East Indies Company in Batavia in December 1702. [ARA.VOC.717]

KENNEDY, GEORGE, born 1714, an Irish Student at the University of Leiden in 1737.   [UL]

KENNEDY, JAMES, from Ireland, married Jannetje Storm from Rotterdam in the Reformed Church there on 23 August 1735. [RA]

KENNEDY, JAMES, born in 1718, an Irish student at the University of Leiden in 1740. [UL]

KENNING, JOHN, from Ireland, married Sara Nieman in the Reformed Church in Amsterdam on 31 October 1651. [AA]

KENOWKETT, CATHERINE, of Bettorar, born 1610, a widow, sailed from Waterford aboard the Angel Gabriel bound for St Malo in France but was storm-damaged and put into Swansea in Wales in 1650. [TNA.HCA.30.853]

KER, JOHN, born 1649, an Irish student of Mathematics at the University of Leiden .   [LU]

KERBY, JOHN, born 1706, an Irish student at the University of Leiden in 1732. [UL]

KERMAN, ARTHUR, an Irish soldier of the Light Horse in Brussels in 1591. [AGRB.34]

KERRIGAN, Private THOMAS, of the 27th [Inniskilling] Regiment, born 1754, fought at the Battle of Waterloo in 1815, and died in 1862.

KILLEY, EDMUND, born 1726, an Irish student at the University of Leiden in 1747. [UL]

KILY, DARBY, from Ireland, married Fansyntje Jans, from Rotterdam in the Reformed Church there on 15 September 1680. [RA]

KINDLEY, PETER, a gentleman from Stensbrigen in the Dukedom of Saxony, was denizised in Ireland on 27 May 1668. [IPR]

KING, ROBERT, born in 1702, an Irish student at the University of Leiden in 1726. [UL]

KIRKPATRICK, ALEXANDER, born 1666, formerly a Colonel of an Irish Regiment under the Duke of Marlborough, died in Longford in 1782. [SM.45.392]

KIRWAN, DAVID, was born in Galway in 1629, son of Edmund Kirwan, David was a merchant in Amsterdam trading between Amsterdam, France and Ireland. [TNA.HCA.3.71.464]

KIRWAN, FRANCIS, master of the John of Galway 60 tons 3 guns, with cargo of Andrew Lynch, a merchant in Galway, with a pass enabling him to sail from Dunkirk to Galway in 1654. [TNA.HCA.14.51.761]

KNOT, EDWARD, born 1708, an Irish student at the University of Leiden in 1732. [UL]

KOOLE, JOHN, a mariner or merchant from Amsterdam, was denizised in Ireland on 23 September 1670. [IPR].

KUSSER, JEEST, reference to in will of Abel De Le Deveze, probate 1749. [PCC]

KUTSER, JOOST, reference to in will of Abel De Le Deveze, probate 1749. [PCC]

LAMBERT, GARRET, master of the Wit Lam van Rotterdam [White Lamb of Rotterdam], when bound from Holland to Dublin, was captured by Robert Clarke, master of the Jocelyn in November 1645. [TNA.HCA.13/63.267]

LAMBERT, JOHN, master of the Fortuin van Duinkerken, [Fortune of Dunkirk] when bound from Nieupoort in Flanders to Ireland was captured by the John of Plymouth Captain Peter Paterson in May 1643. [TNA.HCA.13/246]

LANGSTON, JOHN, born 1672 in Nottingham, a trooper in King William's Army and that of Queen Anne, he fought at Hochster, Malplaquet, and Blenheim, died in Dublin on 12 January 1754. [SM.15.50]

LAUREAN, JOHN, a Sergeant of Colonel John Morphy's Irish Regiment in Flanders from 1646 until 1659. [WG]

LAWLER, DENIS, a Captain of Colonel Owen Roe O'Neill's Irish Regiment in Flanders from 1633 until 1642. [WG]

LAWLER, MARTIN, a Captain of Colonel Dermot O'Sullivan's Irish Regiment in Flanders, from 1646 until 1647; a Captain of Colonel John Morphy's Irish Regiment in Flanders from 1646 until 1659. [WG]

LAWLER, RICHARD, a Captain of Colonel George Cusack's Regiment in the Low Countries from 1656 until 1662. [WG]

LAWRENSON, SIMON, master of the Sampson van Vlissingen, [Simon of Flushing], when bound from Vlissingen to Dublin was captured by the Crescent master Peter Whitty in 1644. [TNA.HCA.13/246]

LAWTON, RICHARD, from Cork, was admitted as a citizen of Rotterdam on 10 March 1768. [RA]

LECKY, JOHN, born in 1707, an Irish student at the University of Leiden in 1727. [UL]

LEE, PETER, born 1660 in Dublin, fought in Flanders, died on Antigua on 8 October 1704. [St John's Cathedral in Antigua]

LEESON, BRYCE, born in 1706, an Irish student at the University of Leiden in 1726. [UL]

LEIGH, FRANCIS, a Lieutenant of MacElligott's Regiment in Flanders around 1688. [IS]

LENNAN, JOHN, an Ensign of Colonel Patrick O'Donnell's Irish Regiment in Flanders from 1643 to 1647. [WG]

LENNOX, WILLIAM, from Cork, was admitted as a citizen of Rotterdam on 8 October 1720. [RA]

LEONARDSON, GEORGE, born 1577, a resident of Youghal, a mariner aboard the Elephant, a 40ton Flemish built ship, was a witness before the High Court of the Admiralty of England in January 1623. [TNA.HCA.13.44.69]

LEONARDSON, LEONARD, from the Netherlands, was denizised in Ireland on 9 October 1623. [IPR]

LERPER, DANIEL GILES, master of the Middelburg of Middelburg from Middelburg in Zeeland bound for Limerick was captured by Thomas Wells, master of the Cat in the River Limerick in 1647. [TNA.HCA.13.62; 15.2.787]

LESLIE, HENRY, born 1689, an Irish student at the University of Leiden in 1709. [UL]

LEYNDEN, JOHN, of Colonel Stanley's Regiment at Spa in 1589. [AGRB.16]

LINCE, OLIVER, , an Ensign of Colonel George Cusack's Regiment in the Low Countries from 1656 until 1662. [WG]

LINDSAY, JOHN, a chaplain of Colonel Patrick O'Donnell's Irish Regiment in Flanders from 1643 to 1647. [WG]

LISCOW, FERGUS, a Captain of Colonel Charles Dillon's Regiment bound for Flanders in 1653; a Captain of Colonel John Morphy's Irish Regiment in Flanders from 1646 until 1659. [WG]

LLOYD, HUGH, born in 1717, an Irish student at the University of Leiden in 1742. [UL]

LLOYD, Dr PHILIP, born 1657, an Anglo-Irish student at Leiden University in 1698. [UL]

LLOYD, THOMAS, born 1709, an Irish student at the University of Leiden from 1735 to 1737. [UL]

LLOYD, TREVOR, born 1701, an Irish student at Leiden University in 1724. [UL]

LOCKWOOD, JOHN, of Colonel Stanley's Regiment at Spa in 1589. [AGRB.16]

LOCKWOOD, ROBERT, born in 1717, an Irish student at the University of Leiden in 1737. [UL]

LOFTUSS, EDMOND, was admitted as a citizen of Rotterdam on 18 September 1709. [RA]

LOGAN, WILLIAM, born 1685, an Irish student at the University of Leiden in 1710. [UL]

LOKINS, JACOB, master of the Abraham was captured by Captain Dankes when bound from Duinkerken [Dunkirk] to Limerick or Wexford in January 1643. [TNA.HCA.13/58.421-430]

51

LOMBERT, JOHN, master of the Fortune of Dunkirk, 40 tons, from Niewpoort in Flanders bound for Ireland with cargo such as St Kitts tobacco, guns and ammunition on behalf of Kacques La Crow of Dunkirk in May 1643. [TNA.HCA13.246/506]

LONORGAN, WILLIAM, an Ensign of Colonel Theodore's Irish Regiment in the Low Countries, 1660-1664. [WG]

LUCAS, DAVID, from Youghal was admitted as a citizen of Rotterdam on 20 January 1720. [RA]

LYNCH, SIMON, born 1710, an Irish student at the University of Leiden in 1750. [UL]

MACAFIE, AENEAS, an Ensign of Colonel John O'Neill's Regiment in Flanders, from 1610 until 1628. [WG]

MACANA, DENIS, a Sergeant of Colonel John O'Neill's Regiment in Flanders, from 1610 until 1628. [WG]

MACANWARD, HUGH BOY, born 1580 in Lettermacaward in Donegal, a Professor of Theology in Leuvan, Brabant, he died in 1635.

MACARRA, CORMACK, an Ensign of Colonel Patrick O'Donnell's Irish Regiment in Flanders from 1643 to 1647. [WG]

MACCARTHY, CHARLES, an Ensign of Colonel Patrick O'Donnell's Irish Regiment in Flanders from 1643 to 1647. [WG]

MACCARTNEY, GEORGE, a merchant in Belfast, a letter to Indocus De La Ville in Brugge, Flanders, dated 29 January 1678, later that year MacCartney sent a consignment of Irish butter on board the Anthony, master Edward Wilson, bound for Ostende in Flanders. [PRONI.MIC.19.2]

MACCARTNEY, Lord's diploma or passport enabling him to travel to the Dutch East Indies, dated 8 March 1793. [PRONI.D2731.5]

MACCARTY, DANIEL, a Sergeant of Colonel James Dempsey's Irish Regiment in the Low Countries from 1660 until 1662. [WG]

MACCARTY, EWAN, born 1723, an Irish student at the University of Leiden in 1748. [UL]

MACCARTY, JAMES, born 1711, an Irish Student at the University of Leiden in 1735. [UL]

MCCARTY, OWEN, a Lieutenant of MacElligott's Regiment in Flanders around 1688. [IS]

MACATEER, EDWARD, born in Ireland, master of a privateer in American service based at Duinkeken, [Dunkirk] during the American Revolutionary War. [MHS]

MACCOIL, MANUS, a Captain of Colonel John Morphy's Irish Regiment in Flanders from 1646 until 1659. [WG]

MCCONACHIE?, [Maconcij], GEORGE, born 1705, an Irish student at the University of Leiden in 1729. [UL]

MCCONNELL, JOHN R., son of George McConnell a merchant in Londonderry, enlisted in the British Army in 1811, a Lieutenant of the 73rd Regiment, was severely wounded at Merxem near Antwerp on 2 February 1814, also severely wounded at the Battle of Waterloo, and died on 23 January 1818 in Ceylon. [2/23.14]

MACDERMODY, MORTAN, a Captain of Colonel John Morphy's Irish Regiment in Flanders from 1646 until 1659. [WG]

MACDERMOT, AMIEL, an Ensign of Colonel John Morphy's Irish Regiment in Flanders from 1646 until 1659. [WG]

MACDERMOT, BERNARD, a Captain of Colonel Thomas Preston's Irish Regiment in Flanders from 1634 until 1641. [WG]

MACDONEL, ALEXANDER, Adjutant of Taafe's Irish Regiment in the Low Countries from 1672 until 1673. [WG]

MACDONAL, JAMES, born in 1716, an Irish student at the University of Leiden in 1737. [UL]

MACDONEL, JOHN, a Captain of Colonel John O'Neill's Regiment in Flanders, from 1610 until 1628. [WG]

MACDONEL, MAURICE, a Captain of Colonel John O'Neill's Regiment in Flanders from 1610 until 1628; a Captain of Colonel Owen Roe O'Neill's Irish Regiment in Flanders from 1633 until 1642; a Captain of Colonel Patrick O'Donnell's Irish Regiment in Flanders from 1643 to 1647. [WG]; was commissioned in Brussels on 18 July 1630. [AGRB]

MACDONAGH, CHARLES, an Ensign of Colonel Theodore's Irish Regiment in the Low Countries, from 1660 until 1664. [WG]

MACDONAGH, EMANUEL, a Captain of Colonel Theodore O'Meara's Irish Regiment in the Low Countries from 1660 to 1664. [WG]

MACDONAGH, FLORENCE, a Captain of Colonel Theodore O'Meara's Irish Regiment in the Low Countries from 1660 to 1664. [WG]

MACDONAGH, MICHAEL, an Ensign of Colonel Theodore's Irish Regiment in the Low Countries, from 1660 until 1664. [WG]

MCDOOL, WILLIAM, from Johnstown, County Donegal, enlisted in the Dutch Brigade, when captured by the French in 1744 he enlisted in the 'Regiment de Clare' at Alost in 1744. [JSAHR.101.406.187]

MACDOWALL, JOHN, born 1688, an Irish student at the University of Leiden in 1709. [UL]

MACELLIGOTT, Captain JOHN, of MacElligott's Regiment in Flanders around 1688. [IS]

MCGEOGHAN, NELLAN, an Ensign of Colonel John O'Neill's Regiment in Flanders, from 1610 until 1628. [WG]

MACGHEE, PATRICK, born 1701, a British- Irish student at Leiden University in 1724. [UL]

MCGILLICUDY, CORNELIUS, a Captain of Colonel Theodore O'Meara's Irish Regiment in the Low Countries from 1660 to 1664. [WG]

MCGILLICUDY, DENIS, Captain Lieutenant of MacElligott's Regiment in Flanders around 1688. [IS]

MCGILLICUDY, DERMOT, an Ensign of Colonel Theodore's Irish Regiment in the Low Countries, 1660-1664. [WG]

MCGILLICUDY, FLORENCE, an Ensign of Colonel James Dempsey's Irish Regiment in the Low Countries from 1660 until 1662. [WG]

MCGILLICUDY, ..., an Ensign of MacEligott's Regiment in Flanders in 1688. [IS]

MACGOWAN, PATRICK, Quartermaster of Colonel James Dempsey's Irish Regiment in the Low Countries from 1660 until 1662. [WG]

MACGRADY, JOHN, a Sergeant of Colonel Patrick O'Donnell's Irish Regiment in Flanders from 1643 to 1647. [WG]

MCGUINNESS, ARTHUR, born 1728, an Irish student at the University of Leiden in 1748. [UL]

MCGUIRE, ALEXANDER, born 25 December 1721 in Newport, Ireland, son of the Baron of Enniskillen, an officer of the Irish Infantry in French Service, fought in Flanders in 1741 and from 1744 until 1748, he retired from the French Army in 1763. [The Jacobite Peerage, Edinburgh, 1904]

MACGUIRE, CAHIR, a Captain of Colonel Philip O'Reilly's Irish Regiment in the Low Countries from 1655 until 1660. [WG]

MCGUIRE, TERENCE, a Captain of Colonel Patrick O'Donnell's Irish Regiment in Flanders from 1643 to 1647. [WG]

MACHAIL, THOMAS, an Ensign of Colonel Patrick O'Donnell's Irish Regiment in Flanders from 1643 to 1647; a Captain of Colonel Patrick O'Donnell's Irish Regiment in Flanders from 1643 to 1647. [WG]

MACHEREL, OWEN, a Sergeant of Colonel John O'Neill's Regiment in Flanders, 1610-1628. [WG]

MACHUGH, CHARLES REILLY, a Captain of Colonel James Dempsey's Irish Regiment in the Low Countries from 1660 until 1662. [WG]

MACHUYER, JOHN REILLY, a Captain of Colonel James Dempsey's Irish Regiment in the Low Countries from 1660 until 1662. [WG]

MACKERIN, JOHN, an Ensign of Colonel John Morphy's Irish Regiment in Flanders from 1646 until 1659. [WG]

MACLEAN, HERMAN, from Ireland, married Ilsbeth Teunis, in the Reformed Church of Rotterdam on 5 November 1628. [RA]

MACLEAR, HUGH, an Ensign of Colonel George Cusack's Regiment in the Low Countries from 1656 until 1662. [WG]

MACLON, THOMAS, from Belfast, married Adriana De Lange, from Ostende, Flanders, in the Presbyterian Church in Rotterdam on 23 October 1726. [RA]

MACMAGON, RODERICK, a Sergeant of Colonel John O'Neill's Regiment in Flanders, from 1610 until 1628. [WG]

MACMAHON, MAURICE, Major of Colonel Dermot O'Sullivan's Irish Regiment in Flanders, from 1646 until 1647. [WG]

MACMAHON, MAURICE, Captain of Colonel Theodore O'Meara's Irish Regiment in the Low Countries from 1660 to 1664; a Captain of Colonel John Murphy's Irish Regiment in the Low Countries from 1667 until 1669. [WG]

MACMILOR, JOHN REILLY, a Captain of Colonel Philip O'Reilly's Irish Regiment in the Low Countries from 1655 until 1660. [WG]

MACMORRIS, ARTHUR, Drum Major of Colonel John O'Neill's Regiment in Flanders, 1610-1628. [WG]

MCMULLAN, Private, of the 27th [Enniskillen] Regiment, born 1780 in County Down, enlisted on 17 January 1814, fought at the Battle of Waterloo in 1815.

MACNAMARA, FELIX, an Ensign of Colonel Theodore's Irish Regiment in the Low Countries, 1660-1664. [WG]

MACNAMARA, REMY, an Ensign of Colonel Theodore's Irish Regiment in the Low Countries, 1660-1664. [WG]

MCNEILL, HECTOR, in Portaferry, owner of the Ann and Sarah of Portaferry entered a charter party with John Wallace, a merchant in Belfast, for a voyage from Belfast to Rotterdam on 28 August 1717. [PRONI.D354.364]

MACRO, MARK, a Captain of Colonel Patrick O'Donnell's Irish Regiment in Flanders from 1643 to 1647. [WG]

MCSWEENY, MAIRUT, an Ensign of Colonel John Morphy's Irish Regiment in Flanders from 1646 until 1659. [WG]

MABBETT, WILLIAM, master of the John of London bound from Barbados to Galway, Limerick or Tralee, was captured by Captain Downes, master of the Hunter in October 1646. [TNA.HCA.13/62]

MADAVAN, Captain, an Irishman, master of the St Francis of Dunkirk, a 100 ton frigate, a privateer, captured the Fortune of Wexford 150 tons bound from Lisbon with a cargo of oil and sugar in 1643. [TNA.HCA.30.863.1158]

MADEN, MICHAEL, from Meath, was admitted as a citizen of Rotterdam on 9 November 1733. [RA]

MADDEN, THOMAS, born 1691, a British-Irish student at Leiden University in 1716. [UL]

MAHON, DENIS, a Captain of Colonel Patrick Fitzgerald's Company in Flanders from 1639 until 1641. [WG]

MAHON, JAMES, an Ensign of Colonel Denis O'Byrne's Irish Regiment in the Low Countries from 1673 until 1686. [IS]

MAHON, MAURICE, a Captain of Colonel Owen Roe O'Neill's Irish Regiment in Flanders from 1633 until 1642. [WG]

MAHONY, Captain JEREMY, of MacElligott's Regiment in Flanders around 1688. [IS]

MANDEVILLE, EDWARD, a Lieutenant of MacElligott's Regiment in Flanders around 1688. [IS]

MANN, ADRIAN, a navigator from Wormer in Holland, was denizised in Ireland on 9 July 1661. [IPR]

MARCHIIS, JACQUES, a merchant from Amsterdam, was denizised in Ireland on 6 September 1608. [IPR]

MARSHALL, LUKE, born 1623 in Wexford, a mariner in Dunkirk from 1638, was bound aboard the John, master Peter Ranssoane, from Dunkirk with a cargo of hops destined for Waterford but was captured by a Parliamentary ship. [TNA.HCA.13.246.526/527]

MARTIN, GEORGE, born 1677, an Irish student at Leiden University in 1697. [AH.59]

MARTINS, JAMES, and his wife Eleanor, from the Netherlands, were naturalized in Ireland on 25 February 1628. [IPR]

MARTIN, JOHN, born 1709, an Irish student at the University of Leiden in 1733. [UL]

MARTIN, JOHN, born 1788 in Armagh, a weaver who enlisted in the 6th [Enniskillen] Dragoons on 7 September 1805, fought at the Battle of

Waterloo, 1815, he served for over twenty-two years when discharged on 2 October 1826. [TNA.WO.]

MARTIN, THOMAS, born 1628, a merchant factor from Galway, settled in Flanders from 1642 until 1646, then in Holland and Zeeland from 1646 until 1652. [TNA.HCA.13.68.450]

MASSIE, JOHN, an Adjutant of Colonel John O'Neill's Regiment in Flanders from 1610 until 1628. [WG]

MATTHEWSON, JORIS, from Ireland, married Geertruyd Jacobs from Rotterdam in the Reformed Church there on 23 September 1698. [RA]

MAULE, JAMES, born in 1706, an Irish student at the University of Leiden in 1726. [UL]

MAULT, DERRICK, master of the Fortune of Ostend, a Danish owned privateer, captured two Scottish ships and sent them to Ostend, however they captured by the Hunter of London then taken to Kinsale for sale in 1646. [TNA.HCA.15.2.1773]

MAXIMILLIAN, ..., a Dutch merchant in Fermanagh in 1809. [PRONI.T1843.8]

MAXWELL, ED., at Berlinghen Camp, in the Netherlands, a letter to Robert Maxwell in Finnebrogue, County Down, dated 10 June 1744. [PRONI.T1023.30]; later at Heer near Maastricht another letter to said Robert Maxwell, dated 5 July 1757. [PRONI]

MEAGH, THADEUS, Quartermaster of Colonel John O'Neill's Regiment in Flanders, 1610-1628. [WG]

MEAGHER, STEPHEN, from Kithenny in Ireland was admitted as a citizen of Rotterdam on 5 September 1718. [RA]

MELLIN, ROBERT, born 1669, an Irish student at Leiden University in 1702. [AH.59]

MERCER, RICHARD, from Dublin, was admitted as a citizen of Rotterdam on 5 January 1758. [RA]

MERRICKE, RICHARD, from Nimegan, Guelderland, in the Netherlands, was naturalised in Ireland on 25 January 1666. [BL.Egerton.77]

METTALLMAN, WILLIAM, master of the Flushing of Flushing [Vlissingen van Vissingen] when Bunratty Castle was held by Parliamentary forces and was besieged by Irish Confederates who pressurised the Dutch to assist but without success in 1646. The Flushing left Limerick with a cargo of tallow, hides, butter, wool, etc but was captured at sea a few days later. [TNA.HCA.13.61.263/]

MICHELLSON, JOHN, from Middelburg, Zealand, was denizised in Ireland on 4 November 1639. [IPR]

MILLER, JAMES, from Dublin, was admitted as a citizen of Rotterdam on 19 April 1720. [RA]

MILLING, ROBERT, born 1678, an Irish student of Theology at Leiden University in 1698. [AH.59]; from Belfast, married Johanna Washington, from Rotterdam, in the Scots Kirk in Rotterdam on 15 February 1712. [RA]

MILLING, ROBERT, born 1690, an Irish student at Leiden University in 1706. [UL]

MITCHELL, HENRY, born in 1707, an Irish student at the University of Leiden in 1727. [UL]

MOLYNEUX, SAMUEL, from Brugge in Vlaanderen, was granted denization in Ireland on 16 August 1594. [IPR]

MOLYNEUX, Sir THOMAS, born in Calais, settled in Bruges, later in Ireland, Chancellor of the Exchequer in Dublin in the reign of Queen Elizabeth. [DPR.232]

MONEY, MATTHEW, a Captain of Colonel John Morphy's Irish Regiment in Flanders from 1646 until 1659. [WG]

MONTGOMERY, JOHN, born 1710, an Irish student at the University of Leiden in 1734. [UL]

MOORE, LAURENCE, a chaplain of MacElligott's Regiment in Flanders in 1688. [IS]

MOORE, PIERCE, born 1713, an Irish student at the University of Leiden in 1736. [UL]

MOORE, SAMUEL, born 1705, an Irish student at the University of Leiden in 1729. [UL]

MORGAN, DERMOT, a Sergeant of Colonel George Cusack's Regiment in the Low Countries from 1656 until 1662. [WG]

MORGAN, ELISABETH, from Dublin, widow of Thomas Waters, married James Gerry from Glasgow, in the Presbyterian Church in Rotterdam, on 15 January 1708. [RA]

MORICE, DUALTACH, a Captain of Colonel John Morphy's Irish Regiment in Flanders from 1646 until 1659. [WG]

MORONY, JOHN, from Limerick, was admitted as a citizen of Rotterdam on 12 May 1719. [RA]

MORPHY JOHN, Colonel of an Irish Regiment in Flanders from 1646 until 1659, and from 1667 until 1669. [WG]

MORRICHE, RICHARD, from Kewmegan in Guelderland, the Netherlands, was denizised in Ireland on 25 January 1667. [IPR]

MORICHE, THADEUS, a Captain of Colonel John Morphy's Irish Regiment in Flanders from 1646 until 1659. [WG]

MORIARITY, DENIS, Adjutant of Colonel John Morphy's Irish Regiment in Flanders from 1646 until 1659. [WG

MORRIS, WILLIAM, Sergeant of an Irish Regiment in Flanders in 1605. [WG]

MORSI, WILLIAM, , an Ensign of Colonel George Cusack's Regiment in the Low Countries from 1656 until 1662. [WG]

MORTOG, MORART, Sergeant of an Irish Regiment in Flanders in 1605. [WG]

MORTLEY, ARTHUR, from Ireland, married Jannetie Van Der Baan, from Rotterdam in the Reformed Church there on 8 November 1648. [RA]

MOSTIN, HUGH, Captain of an Irish Regiment in Flanders in 1605. [WG]

MULCAHEY, TIMOTHY, from Cork, married Lamberdina Hermans, in the Scots Kirk in Rotterdam on 10 October 1744. [RA]

MULLOY, JOHN, born 1706, an Irish student at Leiden University in 1730. [AH.59]

MULRIAN, ANTHONY, Major of Colonel Theodore O'Meara's Irish Regiment in the Low Countries from 1660 to 1664. [WG]

MURPHY, DENIS, a Lieutenant of MacElligott's Regiment in Flanders around 1688. [IS]

MURPHY, HENRY, a Captain of Colonel George Cusack's Regiment in the Low Countries from 1656 until 1662. [WG]

MURPHY, JOHN, a Captain of Colonel George Cusack's Regiment in the Low Countries from 1656 until 1662. [WG]

MURPHY, JOHN, an Ensign of Colonel George Cusack's Regiment in the Low Countries from 1656 until 1662. [WG]

MURPHY, JOHN, a Lieutenant of MacElligott's Regiment in Flanders around 1688. [IS]

MURPHY, PETER, from Cork, married Machteltye Jans, from Elten, in the Reformed Church in Rotterdam, on 5 April 1695. [RA]

MURPHY, PHILIP, an Ensign of Colonel George Cusack's Regiment in the Low Countries from 1656 until 1662. [WG]

MURPHY, PHILIP, an Ensign of MacEligott's Regiment in Flanders in 1688. [IS]

MURPHY, THASEUS, a Captain of Colonel Philip O'Reilly's Irish Regiment in the Low Countries from 1655 until 1660. [WG]

MURRAY, DUDLEY, a Captain of Colonel John Morphy's Irish Regiment in Flanders from 1646 until 1659; a Captain of Colonel George Cusack's Regiment in the Low Countries from 1656 until 1662. [WG]

MUSKET, WILLIAM, born 1716, an Irish student at the University of Leiden in 1745. [UL]

MUSSENDEN, DANIEL, a merchant in Belfast, chartered the Duke of Whitehaven for a voyage from Rotterdam to Belfast in April 1755. [PRONI.D354.570] ; subscribed to a bill of exchange drawn on Joannas Van Somerins in Amsterdam on 25 January 1757. [PRONI.D354/990]

NACHLEN, WILLIAM, a Sergeant of Colonel John O'Neill's Regiment in Flanders, 1610-1628. [WG]

NAPIER, JAMES LENNOX, born in 1717, an Irish student at the University of Leiden in 1737. [UL]

NERBY, RALPH, an Ensign of MacElligott's Regiment in Flanders in 1688. [IS]

NESBIT, ESECHIEL, born 1712, an Irish student at the University of Leiden in 1734. [UL]

NETTERVILLE, EDWARD, born in 1713, an Irish student at the University of Leiden in 1737, an Irish academic at the University of Leiden in 1739. [UL]

NICHOLSON, HENRY, born 1683, a British-Irish student at Leiden University in 1709. [UL]

NICHOLSON, JOHN, born in 1713, an Irish student at the University of Leiden in 1738. [UL]

NICHOLL, JAMES, born 1707, an Irish student at Leiden University in 1731. [UL]

NILIAN, MAURO, an Ensign of Colonel Patrick O'Donnell's Irish Regiment in Flanders from 1643 to 1647. [WG]

NIXON, GEORGE, from Waterford, married Mary Swain, from Waterford, in the Presbyterian Church in Rotterdam on 5 September 1753. [RA]

NOLAN, JAMES, a Captain of Colonel George Cusack's Regiment in the Low Countries from 1656 until 1662. [WG]

NOLAN, NICHOLAS, a Captain of Colonel George Cusack's Regiment in the Low Countries from 1656 until 1662; Adjutant of Colonel Theodore's Irish Regiment in the Low Countries, 1660-1664; a Captain of Colonel Denis O'Byrne's Irish Regiment in the Low Countries from 1673 until 1686. [WG]

NOLAN, ...,, an Ensign of Colonel George Cusack's Regiment in the Low Countries from 1656 until 1662. [WG]

NUGENT, GERALD, of Colonel Stanley's Regiment at Spa in 1589. [AGRB.16]

NUGENT, JAMES, born 1603, a soldier of the Company of Walter Hoid in the Regiment of the Earl of Tyrone, was granted a licence to go to Spain, dated Brussels on 5 January 1631. [AGRB]

NUGENT, JAMES, born 1710, an Irish Student at the University of Leiden in 1734. [UL]

NUGENT, RICHARD, a Captain of Colonel Owen Roe O'Neill's Irish Regiment in Flanders from 1633 until 1642. [WG]

NUGENT, THOMAS, a Captain of Colonel Hugh O'Donnell's Regiment in Flanders from 1632 until 1638. [WG]

O'BOYLE, NELAN, a Captain of Colonel Hugh O'Donnell's Regiment in Flanders from 1632 until 1638. [WG]

O'BRAGAN, DANIEL, a Sergeant of Colonel Hugh O'Donnell's Regiment in Flanders from 1632 until 1638. [WG]

O'BREN, JAMES, an Ensign of Colonel John Morphy's Irish Regiment in Flanders from 1646 until 1659. [WG]

O'BRIAN, ARTHUR, a Captain of Colonel John O'Neill's Regiment in Flanders, 1610-1628, a Captain of Colonel Owen Roe O'Neill's Irish Regiment in Flanders from 1633 until 1642. [WG]

O'BRIN, BERNARD, an Ensign of Colonel Patrick O'Donnell's Irish Regiment in Flanders from 1643 to 1647. [WG]

O'BRIAN, CHARLES, a Captain of Colonel Theodore O'Meara's Irish Regiment in the Low Countries from 1660 to 1664. [WG]

O'BRIEN, CORNELIUS, an Ensign of Colonel Theodore's Irish Regiment in the Low Countries, 1660-1664. [WG]

O'BRIN, DENIS, a Sergeant of Colonel George Cusack's Regiment in the Low Countries from 1656 until 1662. [WG]

O'BRIAN, EDMOND, a Captain of Colonel Owen Roe O'Neill's Irish Regiment in Flanders from 1633 until 1642. [WG]

O'BRIAN, JAMES, a Captain of Colonel John O'Neill's Regiment in Flanders from 1610 until 1628. [WG]

O'BRIAN, MATTHEW, a Captain of Colonel Owen Roe O'Neill's Irish Regiment in Flanders from 1633 until 1642. [WG]

O'BRYEN, Colonel MORTAGH, in 1665, petitioned King Charles II to be employed in Royal service, he claimed that he had fought for King Charles I in Ireland under the Marquis of Ormond and the Marquis of Clanricarde but had moved to Flanders until the Restoration of the Stuart king. [SPIre.]

O'BRIAN, MURROUGH, 6TH Baron Inchiquin, owner of the frigate Darcy based as a privateer at Waterford, was sold by the captain at Dunkirk, but when the ship landed at Amsterdam in 1651, Inchiquin was imprisoned there. [Carte Ms.29.334, Bodleian Library]

O'BRIEN, THEODORE, a Captain of Colonel Theodore O'Meara's Irish Regiment in the Low Countries from 1660 to 1664. [WG]

O'BRIGAN, PATRICK, a Sergeant of Colonel Hugh O'Donnell's Regiment in Flanders from 1632 until 1638. [WG]

O'BRIN, WILLIAM, an Ensign of Colonel John Morphy's Irish Regiment in Flanders from 1646 until 1659; an Ensign of Colonel James Dempsey's Irish Regiment in the Low Countries from 1660 until 1662. [WG]

O'BRIN, WILLIAM, a Sergeant of Colonel Dermot O'Sullivan's Irish Regiment in Flanders, from 1646 until 1647. [WG]

O'BRUN, FELIX, a Captain of Colonel Owen Roe O'Neill's Irish Regiment in Flanders from 1633 until 1642. [WG]

O'BRUYN, HUGH, Sergeant of Colonel Henry O'Neill's Irish Regiment in Flanders in 1605. [WG]

O'BURNIE, DENIS, Major of Colonel John Murphy's Irish Regiment in the Low Countries from 1667 until 1669. [WG]

O'BYRNE, DENIS, Colonel of an Irish Regiment in the Low Countries from 1673 until 1686. [WG]

O'BIRNE, RULIN, of Colonel Stanley's Regiment at Spa in 1589. [AGRB.16]

O'CAHAN, DANIEL, a Captain of Colonel Hugh O'Donnell's Regiment in Flanders from 1632 until 1638. [WG]

O'CALAN, ARTHUR, an Ensign of Colonel Patrick O'Donnell's Irish Regiment in Flanders from 1643 to 1647. [WG]

O'CALAN, MALACHY, a Captain of Colonel John Morphy's Irish Regiment in Flanders from 1646 until 1659. [WG]

O'CALLANAN, FLORENCE, Chief Surgeon of Colonel John O'Neill's Regiment in Flanders, 1610-1628. [WG]

O'CASEY, DERMOT, a Sergeant of Colonel John Morphy's Irish Regiment in Flanders from 1646 until 1659. [WG]

O'CHARARULA, PATRICK, an Ensign of Colonel Patrick O'Donnell's Irish Regiment in Flanders from 1643 to 1647. [WG]

O'CONNELL, CONNELL, born 1700 in Cork, for 20 years was in the service of the Prince of Orange, was promoted to the rank of Colonel in the Dutch Army in 1768, died on 24 January 1783. [IG.9.3.404]

O'CONNELL, CONNER, born 1724, an Irish student at the University of Leiden in 1746. [UL]

O'CONNOR, OWEN, from Connaught, served in the Duke of Gloucester's Legion in the Low Countries until the surrender of Duinkerken [Dunkirk] , petitioned King Charles II for a pass, which was granted on 15 August 1663. [SPIre]

O'CONNOR, PHILIP, an Ensign of Colonel Denis O'Byrne's Irish Regiment in the Low Countries from 1673 until 1686. [WG]

O'CONNOR, THOMAS, Drum-major of Colonel John O'Neill's Regiment in Flanders, 1610-1628. [WG]

O'CONNOR, CONMAC ROS, of Colonel Stanley's Regiment at Spa in 1589. [AGRB.16]

O'DALY, CHARLES, a Captain of Colonel Thomas Preston's Irish Regiment in Flanders from 1634 until 1641. [WG]

O'DALY, DANIEL, was commissioned as Captain of Irish infantry in the Earl of Tyrone's Regiment, dated Brussels 21 September 1630. [AGRB]

O'DALY, DANIEL. a Captain of Colonel Hugh O'Donnell's Regiment in Flanders from 1632 until 1638.

O'DANIEL, JOHN, a Captain of Colonel Patrick O'Donnell's Irish Regiment in Flanders from 1643 to 1647. [WG]

O'DANIEL, JOHN, from Limerick, a privateer based in Dunkirk in 1642. [HMC.Franciscan.132]

O'DENSI, DENSI, an Ensign of Colonel Patrick O'Donnell's Irish Regiment in Flanders from 1643 to 1647. [WG]

O'DENSI, DENSI, a Captain of Colonel Patrick O'Donnell's Irish Regiment in Flanders from 1643 to 1647. [WG]

O'DENSI, DERMOT, a Captain of Colonel Patrick O'Donnell's Irish Regiment in Flanders from 1643 to 1647. [WG]

O'DEORAN, DANIEL, Ensign of Taafe's Irish Regiment in the Low Countries from 1672 until 1673. [WG]

O'DONAHUE, EDMOND, chaplain of Colonel Henry O'Neill's Irish Regiment in Flanders in 1605. [WG]

O'DOHERTY, MANUS, Sergeant of Colonel Henry O'Neill's Irish Regiment in Flanders in 1605. [WG]

O'DONNELL, CONSTANTINE, a Captain of Colonel Denis O'Byrne's Irish Regiment in the Low Countries from 1673 until 1686. [WG]

O'DONNELL, DANIEL, a chaplain of Colonel Patrick O'Donnell's Irish Regiment in Flanders from 1643 to 1647. [WG]

O'DONNELL. HENRY, a Captain of Colonel George Cusack's Regiment in the Low Countries from 1656 until 1662. [WG]

O'DONNELL, HUGH, born 1600, son of the Earl of Tyrconnell, moved to Flanders in 1607, enlisted in the Spanish Army in 1657, Colonel of an Irish Regiment in Flanders from 1632 to 1638, he was killed by the French in 1642.

O'DONELL, JAMES, a Captain of Colonel John Morphy's Irish Regiment in Flanders from 1646 until 1659. [WG]

O'DONNELL, JOHN, a Captain of Colonel John Morphy's Irish Regiment in Flanders from 1646 until 1659. [WG]

O'DONNEL, PATRICK, an Ensign of Colonel John O'Neill's Regiment in Flanders, 1610-1628; Colonel of an Irish Regiment in Flanders from 1643 to 1647. [WG]

66

O'DONELL, ROBERT, Captain of Irish infantry, an order dated Brussels on 21 July 1630. [AGRB]

O'DONNELLY, HENRY, Adjutant of Colonel Theodore's Irish Regiment in the Low Countries, 1660-1664. [WG]

O'DRISCOLL, DERMOT, a Sergeant of Colonel John O'Neill's Regiment in Flanders, 1610-1628. [WG]

O'DUGAN, JOHN, a Sergeant of Colonel Hugh O'Donnell's Regiment in Flanders from 1632 until 1638. [WG]

O'DUIR, WILLIAM, an Ensign of Colonel Denis O'Byrne's Irish Regiment in the Low Countries from 1673 until 1686. [WG]

O'DWYER, JOHN, Quartermaster of Colonel Theodore's Irish Regiment in the Low Countries, 1660-1664. [WG]

O'DWYER, PHILIP, a Captain of Colonel Theodore O'Meara's Irish Regiment in the Low Countries from 1660 to 1664. [WG]

O'DWYER, ..., a Captain of Colonel Denis O'Byrne's Irish Regiment in the Low Countries from 1673 until 1686. [WG]

O'FARRELL, FERGUS, a Captain of Colonel Philip O'Reilly's Irish Regiment in the Low Countries from 1655 until 1660; a Captain of Colonel John Morphy's Irish Regiment in Flanders from 1646 until 1659; a Captain of Colonel George Cusack's Regiment in the Low Countries from 1656 until 1662. [WG]

O'FARRELL, GERARD, Chaplain of Colonel John Murphy's Irish Regiment in the Low Countries from 1667 until 1669. [WG]

O'FAY, MARTIN, a Sergeant of Colonel John Morphy's Irish Regiment in Flanders from 1646 until 1659. [WG]

O'GAN, JAMES, of Colonel Stanley's Regiment at Spa in 1589. [AGRB.16]

O'GALLAGHER, TERENCE, a Captain of Colonel Thomas Preston's Irish Regiment in Flanders from 1634 until 1641; a Captain of Colonel Patrick O'Donnell's Irish Regiment in Flanders from 1643 to 1647. [WG]

O'HAGAN, HENRY, an Ensign of Colonel John O'Neill's Regiment in Flanders, 1610-1628. [WG]

67

O'HARE, CAHIR, Adjutant of Colonel Philip O'Reilly's Irish Regiment in the Low Countries from 1655 until 1660. [WG]

O'HAUGHERNE, Captain SIMON, of MacElligott's Regiment in Flanders around 1688. [IS]

O'HAY, GEORGE, an Ensign of Colonel Patrick O'Donnell's Irish Regiment in Flanders from 1643 to 1647. [WG]

O'HAY, PHILIP, a Captain of Colonel Patrick O'Donnell's Irish Regiment in Flanders from 1643 to 1647. [WG]

O'HEA, EWAN, an Adjutant of Colonel Denis O'Byrne's Irish Regiment in the Low Countries from 1673 until 1686. [WG]

O'HIGNY, THADEUS, a Sergeant of Colonel Patrick O'Donnell's Irish Regiment in Flanders from 1643 to 1647. [WG]

O'KELLY, JOHN, an Ensign of Colonel John Murphy's Irish Regiment in the Low Countries from 1667 until 1669. [WG]

O'KELLY, JOHN, Quartermaster of Colonel John Murphy's Irish Regiment in the Low Countries from 1667 until 1669. [WG]

O'KELLY, THADEUS, a Captain of Colonel Owen Roe O'Neill's Irish Regiment in Flanders from 1633 until 1642. [WG] in 1633 he was commissioned in Brussels to recruit soldiers for Colonel Ewan O'Neill. [AGRB.1234]

O'KENNEDY, DENIS, a Sergeant of Colonel Hugh O'Donnell's Regiment in Flanders from 1632 until 1638. [WG]

O'KENNEDY, MAURICE, of Colonel John Morphy's Irish Regiment in Flanders from 1646 until 1659. [WG]

O'LEANNAIN, DANIEL, a Captain of Colonel George Cusack's Regiment in the Low Countries from 1656 until 1662. [WG]

O'LEARY, PATRICK, born 1776 in Tralee, County Kerry, a soldier of the Kerry Militia, enlisted in the British Army on 9 December 1809, a Colour Sergeant of the 73rd Regiment of Foot, was wounded at the Battle of Waterloo and was discharged on 27 February 1816. [2/73.170]

O'MAHON, DANIEL, an Ensign of Colonel John O'Neill's Regiment in Flanders, 1610-1628. [WG]

O'MAHON, DANIEL, an Ensign in the Regiment of the Earl of Tyrone, was commissioned as Captain of the said regiment, in Brussels on 17 January 1631. [AGRB]

O'MALLY, BERNARD, a Sergeant of Colonel Patrick O'Donnell's Irish Regiment in Flanders from 1643 to 1647. [WG]

O'MEARA, ALEXANDER, a Captain of Colonel Theodore O'Meara's Irish Regiment in the Low Countries from 1660 to 1664. [WG]

O'MEARA, DENIS, an Ensign of Colonel Theodore's Irish Regiment in the Low Countries, 1660-1664. [WG]

O'MEARA, THEODORE, Colonel of an Irish Regiment in the Low Countries from 1660 to 1664. [WG]

O'MOLEDI, CHARLES, a Captain of Colonel John Morphy's Irish Regiment in Flanders from 1646 until 1659. [WG]

O'MORROW, MALACHY, an Ensign of Colonel John O'Neill's Regiment in Flanders, 1610-1628; a Captain of Colonel Owen Roe O'Neill's Irish Regiment in Flanders from 1633 until 1642. [WG]

O'MULLOAGHLYN, NEILLAN, Captain of Colonel Henry O'Neill's Irish Regiment in Flanders in 1605. [WG]

O'MULRIAN, ANTHONY, Captain of a company of Irish infantry, a grant of thirty crowns, dated in Brussels on 12 July 1630. [AGRB]

O'MULRAIN, CHARLES, a Captain of Colonel Theodore O'Meara's Irish Regiment in the Low Countries from 1660 to 1664; a Captain of Colonel Denis O'Byrne's Irish Regiment in the Low Countries from 1673 until 1686. [WG]

O'MULRIAN, EDMUND, an Ensign of Colonel Theodore's Irish Regiment in the Low Countries, 1660-1664. [WG]

O'MULRIAN, EWAN, a Captain of Colonel John O'Neill's Regiment in Flanders, 1610- 1628; a Captain of Colonel Hugh O'Donnell's Regiment in Flanders from 1632 until 1638. [WG]

O'NEALE, ROBERT WILLIAM, born 16 June 1833, a merchant in Bridgetown, Barbados late Consul for the Netherlands, died 15 February 1879. [St Michael's Cathedral , Bridgetown, gravestone]

O'NEILL, ARTHUR, Captain of Colonel Henry O'Neill's Irish Regiment in Flanders in 1605. [WG]

O'NEILL, ARTHUR, Major of Colonel Owe Roe O'Neill's Regiment in Flanders from 1633 until 1642. [WG]

O'NEILL, BERNARD, a Captain of Colonel Owen Roe O'Neill's Irish Regiment in Flanders from 1633 until 1642. [WG]

O'NEILL, CHARLES, an Ensign of Colonel John O'Neill's Regiment in Flanders, from 1610 until 1628. [WG]

O'NEILL, CONSTANTINE, a Captain of Colonel Owen Roe O'Neill's Irish Regiment in Flanders from 1633 until 1642; a Captain of Colonel Philip O'Reilly's Irish Regiment in the Low Countries from 1655 until 1660. [WG]

O'NEILL, DANIEL, fought at the Siege of Breda in 1637, in exile in Europe between 1641 and 1658; an Irish exile at the Stuart Courts in the Netherlands. [SH.4.104-133; SH.5.42-76]

O'NEILL, EWAN, Captain of Colonel Henry O'Neill's Irish Regiment in Flanders in 1605. [WG]

O'NEILL, HENRY, recruited a regiment in Ireland for service in Flanders in 1604, Colonel of a regiment of Irish soldiers in Flanders from 1605 until 1609, when he moved to Spain where he died on 25 August 1610. [WG]

O'NEILL, HENRY, a Captain of Colonel Owen Roe O'Neill's Irish Regiment in Flanders from 1633 until 1642. [WG]

O'NEILL, HUGH, an Adjutant of Colonel John O'Neill's Regiment in Flanders, 1610-1628. [WG]

O'NEILL, HENRY, a Captain of Colonel Owen Roe O'Neill's Irish Regiment in Flanders from 1633 until 1642. [WG]

O'NEILL, JOHN, nephew of the Earl of Tyrone and the Irish Regiment in Spanish service in Flanders, dated 9 February 1616. [NLI]

O'NEILL, JOHN, a Captain of Colonel Owen Roe O'Neill's Irish Regiment in Flanders from 1633 until 1642. [WG]

O'NEILL, NELAN, a Captain of Colonel Owen Roe O'Neill's Irish Regiment in Flanders from 1633 until 1642. [WG]

O'NEILL, OWEN ROE, Colonel of an Irish Regiment in Flanders from 1633 when he and his regiment were shipped from Flanders to Ireland aboard the Flemish frigate St Francis, a 200 ton frigate, in July 1642.

O'NEILL, PATRICK, an Ensign of Colonel George Cusack's Regiment in the Low Countries from 1656 until 1662. [WG]

O'NEILL, PHILIP, a chaplain of Colonel Owen Roe O'Neill's Irish Regiment in Flanders from 1633 until 1642. [WG]

O'NEILL, TERENCE, an Ensign of Colonel Denis O'Byrne's Irish Regiment in the Low Countries from 1673 until 1686. [WG]

O'NULAN, JAMES, a Captain of Colonel James Dempsey's Irish Regiment in Low Countries from 1660 until 1662. [WG]

O'QUILLY, EDMOND, a drum major of Colonel Owen Roe O'Neill's Irish Regiment in Flanders from 1633 until 1642. [WG]

O'QUINN, JOHN, a Captain of Colonel Theodore O'Meara's Irish Regiment in the Low Countries from 1660 to 1664. [WG]

O'REILLY, EWAN, a Captain of Colonel John O'Neill's Regiment in Flanders, 1610-1628. [WG]

O'REILLY, FERDINAND, an Ensign of Colonel John O'Neill's Regiment in Flanders, 1610-1628. [WG]

O'REILLY, HUGH, a Captain of Colonel John O'Neill's Regiment in Flanders, 1610-1628. [WG]

O'REILLY, HUGH, an Ensign of Colonel James Dempsey's Irish Regiment in the Low Countries from 1660 until 1662. [WG]

O'REILLY, JOHN, a Captain Colonel of an Irish Regiment in the Low Countries from 1655 until 1660. [WG]

O'REILLY, PHILIP, Colonel of an Irish Regiment in the Low Countries from 1655 until 1660. [WG]

O'RIERDAN, DANIEL, born 1608, a soldier in the Company of Captain Gerald Maurice in the Earl of Tyrone's Regiment, a licence to return to Ireland for one year, dated Brussels 23 March 1630. [AGRB]

O'SHERIDAN, TERENCE, a soldier in the Company of Captain Thadeus O'Sullivan, a licence to return to Ireland, dated Brussels 23 February 1630. [AGRB]

O'SHIEL, CHARLES, a Captain of Colonel John Morphy's Irish Regiment in Flanders from 1646 until 1659. [WG]

O'SHIEL, EWAN, doctor of Colonel John O'Neill's Regiment in Flanders, 1610-1628; doctor of the Earl of Tyron's Regiment at Mechelen in 1631 [AGRB]; a Captain of Colonel Owen Roe O'Neill's Irish Regiment in Flanders from 1633 until 1642. [WG]

O'SULLIVAN, CORNELIUS, a soldier in the Company of Captain Dermot O'Sullivan in the Regiment of the Earl of Tyrone, a grant of four crowns, dated 8 November 1630. [AGRB]

O'SULLIVAN, DERMOT, a Captain of Colonel John O'Neill's Regiment in Flanders, 1610-1628; Major of Colonel Patrick O'Donnell's Irish Regiment in Flanders from 1643 to 1647. [WG]

O'SULLIVAN MOR, DERMOT, in the Spanish Army by 1627, Colonel of an Irish Regiment in Flanders from 1646 until 1647. [WG]

O'SULLIVAN, PHILIP, a Captain of Colonel Dermot O'Sullivan's Irish Regiment in Flanders, from 1646 until 1647. [WG]

O'SULLIVAN, THADEUS, a former Captain of the Earl of Tyron's Regiment, was granted a monthly pension of 40 Crowns in 1632. [AGRB.1227]

OLFERTS, BAUKE, a mariner from Cowdum in Friesland, was denisized in Ireland on 10 July 1675. [IPR]

OLFERTS, DOWE, a mariner from Cowdum in Friesland, was denisized in Ireland on 10 July 1675. [IPR]

OLFERTES, WYBRAND, born in Holland, was naturalised in Ireland on 6 February 1618. [IPR]

OLIVER, FRANCIS, master of the privateer Patrick of Wexford attacked the Adventure near the Scilly Isles in 1647. [TNA. HCA.13.248]

ORMOND,........, from Ireland to Caen, France, in 1650.

ORMOND, MARGARET, in Brugge, Vlandaaren, a letter dated 20 September 1656. [NLI]

72

PANKART, JACOB, from Zealand, was the factor in Dublin for Adrian and Cornelius Lampson, merchants in Rotterdam, around 1645. [TNA.HCA.13.58.161/165]; he loaded goods aboard the Blessing in Dublin in May 1645 for shipment to Isaac Paulson and Jacob Pankart in Holland. [TNA.HCA.13.58.167]

PATERSON, JOHN, master of the Red Fortune of Amsterdam, was captured by the Assurance near Blasket Isle in July 1647 when bound from Galway to France. [TNA.HCA.15.2]

PATRICK, JOHN, a Captain of Colonel Theodore O'Meara's Irish Regiment in the Low Countries from 1660 to 1664, Captain of Colonel John Murphy's Irish Regiment in the Low Countries from 1667 until 1669; Major of Taafe's Irish Regiment in the Low Countries from 1672 until 1673. [WG]

PATRICK, THADEUS MACGRILES, a Captain of Colonel John Morphy's Irish Regiment in Flanders from 1646 until 1659. [WG]

PAUL, JOSHUA, born in 17094, an Irish student at the University of Leiden in 1729. [UL]

PAULSON, ISAAC, a merchant in Rotterdam trading with Dublin around 1639-1645, freighted the Blessing, master Charles Cant, for two voyages. [TNA.HCA.13.59.161]

PEACOCK, JAMES, master of the Tiger captured the Rose Crane of Amsterdam when bound from Galway to Vlissingen [Flushing] in April 1649. [TNA.HCA13.250.II]; he also captured the Zwalou van Vlissingen [Swallow of Flushing] master Francis Martyn in April 1649 when bound from Flushing to Dungarvan. [TNA.HCA.13.61.400]; plus the Cornelius of Wexford, master Clement van der Ryder, in November 1649. [TNA.HCA13/50.1]

PEACOCK, MARMADUKE, from Limerick, was admitted as a citizen of Rotterdam on 23 December 1720. [RA]

PEACOCK, UPTON, born 1695, an Irish student at Leiden University in 1714. [UL]

PENN, WILLIAM, Captain of the Assurance, captured the St Francis of St Malo bound for Galway in February 1648, also the St James of Newhaven with a cargo of salt, tobacco, etc bound for Limerick or Galway. [TNA.HCA.15.2]

PERCIVAL, WILLIAM in Dublin, a letter to Dr Robert Percival in Leiden, dated 22 July 1780. [PRONI.D906.162]

PERRY, MICAJAH, born 1692, an Irish student at the University of Leiden in 1712-1715. [UL]

PETERSON, CHRISTOPHER, from Alkmaar in Holland, was denizised in Ireland on 11 December 1655. [IPR]

PETERSOUN, CHRISTOPHER, a merchant from Holland, was denizised in Ireland on 17 February 1662. [IPR]

PETERSON, CORNELIUS, boatswain of the Rosecrane of Amsterdam with 180 Irish soldiers bound from Galway for Vlissingen in 1649 but was captured by a Parliamentary frigate, the Tiger's Whelp, and taken to Milford Haven in Wales in April 1649. [TNA.HCA.13.250]

PETERSON, GARRET, master of the Fortuin van Duinkerken [Fortune of Dunkirk], when bound from Duinkerken to Ireland in December 1644 was captured by the Warwick, a frigate, master William Thomas. [TNA.HCA.13/247]

PHIBBS, Lieutenant Colonel ORMSBY, of the 118th Regiment, [the Connaught Rangers] died of yellow fever on 17 January 1848. [St Paul's gravestone, Barbados]

PICKOTT, GEORGE, from Dublin, was admitted as a citizen of Rotterdam on 1 May 1762. [RA]

PIERS, HENRY, from Dublin, was admitted as a citizen of Rotterdam on 27 March 1741. [RA]

PIKE, JOHN, born in 1695, an Anglo-Irish student at the University of Leiden in 1728. [UL]

PILE, MARIA, from Dublin, was admitted as a citizen of Rotterdam on 13 September 1717. [RA]

PLATT, HENRY, a Captain of Colonel Denis O'Byrne's Irish Regiment in the Low Countries from 1673 until 1686. [WG]

PLUNKETT, BARTHOLEMEW, a chaplain of Colonel Patrick O'Donnell's Irish Regiment in Flanders from 1643 to 1647; a Sergeant of Colonel George Cusack's Regiment in the Low Countries from 1656 until 1662. [WG]

PLUNKETT, CHRISTOPHER, a Captain of Colonel Patrick O'Donnell's Irish Regiment in Flanders from 1643 to 1647. [WG]

PLUNKETT, CHRISTOPHER, an Ensign of Colonel Patrick O'Donnell's Irish Regiment in Flanders from 1643 to 1647; a Captain of Colonel John Morphy's Irish Regiment in Flanders from 1646 until 1659. [WG]

PLUNKETT, JAMES, a Captain of Colonel Owen Roe O'Neill's Irish Regiment in Flanders from 1633 until 1642. [WG]

PLUNKETT, Captain MAURICE, of MacElligott's Regiment in Flanders from 1668 until 1689. [IS]

PLUNKETT, NICHOLAS, of Dunshaughlin, in 1667, petitioned King Charles II, stating that he had fought for the king and Charles I in Ireland and in Flanders under the Duke of Ormond. [SPIre]

PLUNKETT, Captain PATRICK, sr., of the Grenadier Company, in MacElligott's Regiment in Flanders from 1668 until 1689. [IS]

PLUNKETT, PATRICK, jr., Captain of MacElligott's Regiment in Flanders around 1688. [IS]

PLUNKETT, RICHARD, a Major of Colonel Thomas Preston's Irish Regiment in Flanders from 1634 until 1641. [WG]

PLUNKETT, THOMAS, a Captain of Colonel John O'Neill's Regiment in Flanders, from 1610 to 1628, a Captain of Colonel Owen Roe O'Neill's Irish Regiment in Flanders from 1633 until 1642. [WG]

PLUNKETT, THOMAS, master of the Discovery, when bound from La Rochelle in France for Dublin, was seized by the Angel of Amsterdam master Adrian Franson, in June 1645, also the Spiegel van Duinkerken [Mirror of Dunkirk] was seized at Waterford Harbour in November 1649. [TNA.HCA.3.20]; master of the Mirror of Dunkirk, a privateer, captured several English ships in July 1649.

PLUNKETT, WILLIAM, of the Company of Captain Mauro Mahon in the Earl of Tyrone's Regiment, an order dated Brussels on 23 May 1631. [AGRB]

POER, MAURICE, an Ensign of MacElligott's Regiment in Flanders in 1688. [IS]

POER, WILLIAM, Ensign of MacElligott's Regiment in Flanders in 1688. [IS]

PONSONBY, JOHN, born 1714, an Irish Student at the University of Leiden in 1734. [UL]

PORDY, ROBERT, Quartermaster of Colonel Owen Roe O'Neill's Irish Regiment in Flanders from 1633 until 1642. [WG]

PORTELOS, MICHAEL, Surgeon of MacElligott's Regiment in Flanders in 1688. [IS]

POWER, BERNARD, born 1648, from Ireland, a student of Philosophy at Leiden University in 1668. [AH.59]

POWER, JAMES, a Captain of Colonel Thomas Preston's Irish Regiment in Flanders from 1634 until 1641. [WG]

POWER, JAMES, a student, son of Robert Power a merchant in Francis Street, Dublin, died in Tournai, Flanders, in May 1770. [FLJ.43]

POWER, RICHARD, born 1704, an Irish student at Leiden University in 1724. [UL]

POYNTZ, ELIZABETH, daughter of Daniel Poyntz, was baptised in St Bride's, Dublin, on 30 August 1670.

PRATT, JOSEPH, born 1668, an Irish student at the University of Leiden in 1688. [UL]

PRATT, JOSEPH, an Anglo-Irish academic at the University of Leiden in 1692. [UL]

PRENDERGAST, JAMES, a Lieutenant of MacElligott's Regiment in Flanders around 1688. [IS]

PRESTON, JAMES, a Captain of Colonel Hugh O'Donnell's Regiment in Flanders from 1632 until 1638, a Captain of Colonel Thomas Preston's Irish Regiment in Flanders from 1634 until 1641. [WG]

PRESTON, ROBERT, a Captain of Colonel Thomas Preston's Irish Regiment in Flanders from 1634 until 1641. [WG]

PRESTON, THOMAS, Captain of Colonel Henry O'Neill's Irish Regiment in Flanders in 1605. [WG]

PRESTON, THOMAS, a Major of Colonel Hugh O'Donnell's Regiment in Flanders from 1632 until 1638; Colonel of an Irish Regiment, in Flanders from 1634 until 1641, returned to Ireland in 1642. [WG]

PRUNCAS, ..., master of the Patrick of Wexford, 160 tons, a privateer in the 1640s. [MM.76.123]

PURCELL, PHILIP, an Ensign of Colonel John O'Neill's Regiment in Flanders, 1610-1628, a Captain of Colonel Owen Roe O'Neill's Irish Regiment in Flanders from 1633 until 1642. [WG]

PURDON, GILBERT, born 1700, an Irish student at Leiden University in 1722. [UL]

PURDON, JOHN, born 1710, an Irish student at Leiden University in 1731. [UL]

PURDON, SIMON, born 1694, an Irish student at Leiden University in 1717. [UL]

PURCELL, PETER, a Captain of Colonel James Dempsey's Irish Regiment in the Low Countries from 1660 until 1662. [WG]

QUICKELIMBER, LEWIS, a merchant in Amsterdam trading with Limerick in 1648, with cargo for John Peterson in Galway. [TNA.HCA.13.249]

RANDAL, Captain of the privateer Patrick of Wexford attacked the Adventure near the Scilly Isles in 1647. [TNA. HCA.13.248]

RATHE, DENIS, an Ensign of Colonel John O'Neill's Regiment in Flanders, 1610-1628 . [WG]

RATH, JOHN, Captain of Colonel Henry O'Neill's Irish Regiment in Flanders in 1605. [WG]

READ, WILLIAM, born 1716, an Irish student at the University of Leiden in 1749. [UL]

READMUN, HENRY, a mariner on the privateer Michael of Wexford which attacked the Richard of Bristol off Land's End, England in August 1648. [TNA.HCA.13.249]

REILLY, BERNARD, an Ensign of Colonel John Morphy's Irish Regiment in Flanders from 1646 until 1659. [WG]

REILLY, CHARLES, a Captain of Colonel Philip O'Reilly's Irish Regiment in the Low Countries from 1655 until 1660.

REILLY, EDMUND, a Captain of Colonel Philip O'Reilly's Irish Regiment in the Low Countries from 1655 until 1660; a Captain of Colonel James Dempsey's Irish Regiment in the Low Countries from 1660 until 1662. [WG]

REILLY, EDMOND, Drum Major of Colonel James Dempsey's Irish Regiment in the Low Countries from 1660 until 1662. [WG]

REILLY, EWAN, a Sergeant of Colonel James Dempsey's Irish Regiment in the Low Countries from 1660 until 1662. [WG]

REILLY, JOHN, an Ensign of Colonel James Dempsey's Irish Regiment in the Low Countries from 1660 until 1662, also an Ensign of Colonel John Murphy's Irish Regiment in the Low Countries from 1667 until 1669. [WG]

REILLY, PHILIP, a Captain of Colonel James Dempsey's Irish Regiment in the Low Countries from 1660 until 1662. [WG]

REILLY, TERENCE, Adjutant of Colonel Philip O'Reilly's Irish Regiment in the Low Countries from 1655 until 1660; an Adjutant of Colonel James Dempsey's Irish Regiment in the Low Countries from 1660 until 1662. [WG]

REIJNET [?], JAMES, born 1696, an Irish student at Leiden University in 1714.[UL]

RICE, JAMES, born 1690, an Anglo-Irish student at Leiden University from 1715 until 1718. [UL]

RICH, MARCUS, born 1618, a merchant of Limerick, trading in Holland and Zealand in 1648. [TNA.HCA.13.249]

RICHARD, JAMES, an Irish soldier of Colonel Stanley's Regiment in Brussels in 1590. [AGRB.28]

RICHARDSON, HENRY, born 1709, an Irish Student at the University of Leiden in 1733; an Irish academic at the University of Leiden in 1735. [UL]

RICHARDSON, WILLIAM, born 1695, an Irish student at Leiden University in 1720. [UL]

RICKMAN, JAMES, born in the Netherlands, a perfumer in the parish of St Keven in Dublin was naturalised in Ireland on 12 July 1641. [IPR]

RIDDY, RICHARD, born in 1716, an Irish student at the University of Leiden in 1743, an Irish academic at the University of Leiden in 1745. [UL]

RIDGATE, PHILIP, an Irish student at the University of Utrecht in 1701. [UU]

RILER, MILER, a Captain of Colonel James Dempsey's Irish Regiment in the Low Countries from 1660 until 1662. [WG]

RILHAN, ANTHONY, born in 1718, an Irish student at the University of Leiden in 1740. [UL]

RINGROSE, RICHARD, born 1700, an Irish student at Leiden University in 1722. [UL]

ROBERTS, THOMAS, born 1695, an Irish student at Leiden University in 1715.[UL]

ROBERTSON, WILLIAM, from Dublin, a soldier in Dutch Service was bound from the Netherlands to the West Indies aboard the White Swan, an inventory dated 1638. [Old Notarial Accounts, Rotterdam Inventories.293]

ROBINSON, ARTHUR, born 1706, an Irish Student at the University of Leiden in 1733. [UL]

ROCHE, ADAM, a Captain of Colonel John Morphy's Irish Regiment in Flanders from 1646 until 1659. [WG]

ROCHE, DAVID, a Captain of Colonel John Morphy's Irish Regiment in Flanders from 1646 until 1659. [WG]

ROCH, MARK, master of the Eagle of Limerick, owned by James Ronane, Nicholas Ronane, Francis Rice, Lawrence Rice, Bartholemew Rice, Edward Gold, and John Casy, all merchants in Limerick, with a cargo of butter wool, and tallow, bound for Morris Roch, William Lea, and Richard Trant, Irish merchants in La Rochelle, sailed from Limerick on 7 December 1649 but was seized near Cardiff. Aboard the Eagle were Irish passengers, including Edward Elcock, a mercer from Drogherda, Christoper Charles a priest from Limmeioke in County Waterford, Edmund Purcell, a merchant from Waterford, Katherine Collins, wife f Collando Collett, late a barber surgeon in Wexford, also Peter Wise from Waterford, the boatswain of the Eagle. [TNA.HCA.13. 250.667]

ROCQUITTE, and VAN TEYLINGEN in Rotterdam, in correspondence with Daniel Mussenden in Belfast on 4 October 1757. [PRONI.D354.995]

ROE, DOMINICK, Major of Colonel George Cusack's Regiment in the Low Countries from 1656 until 1662. [WG]

ROE, FRANCIS, born in Cork, was captured when aboard the privateer 'Caesar of Cowes', enlisted in the Company of Captain Murtagh O'Brian of Clare's Regiment in French Service, in 1740s. [JSAHR.101.406.188]

ROE, JOHN, born 1684, an Irish student of Law at Leiden University in 1704. [AH.59]

ROE, WILLIAM, born 1682, from Cork, an Irish student at Leiden University in 1704. [AH.59]

ROE, WILLIAM, from Tipperary, an Irish academic at Utrecht University in 1708. [UU]

ROGERS, GEORGE, an Anglo-Irish student at the University of Utrecht in 1705-1708. [UU]

ROGERSON, JOHN, a merchant from Rotterdam, in Holland, was denizized in Ireland on 15 April 1673. [IPR]

ROHART, THEODORE, from Lille in Flanders, was naturalised in Ireland on 4 November 1639. [IPR]

RONCEN, THOMAS, an Irish soldier in Flanders in 1589. [AGRB,13]

ROOTH, FRANCIS, from Wexford, died in Lovaine, Brabant, probate 1692, Prerogative Court of Canterbury. [TNA]

ROSE, WILLIAM, of Nieuwpoort in Flanders, a passenger aboard the Fortune of Dunkirk from Dunkirk bound for Ireland in May 1643. [TNA.HCA.13.246.507]

ROSSITER, JOHN, master of an Irish man o'war from Wexford, captured the Pieter van Rotterdam, 60 tons, owned by John Lennekyn of Rotterdam, when bound from Rotterdam with a cargo of rye bound for Bristol, which was then taken to Waterford on 19 May 1648. [TNA.HCA.13.58.278]; on 19 May 1648, John Rossiter captured the Hope of Amsterdam, [owners

Pieter Jacobson Nyen and John Beten] master Swar Swartson, born 1613, from Der Schelling in Holland, which was taken as a prize to Waterford. [TNA.HCA.13.58.279/281]

ROST, WILLIAM, a Captain of Colonel John Morphy's Irish Regiment in Flanders from 1646 until 1659. [WG]

ROSS, DERMOT, Sergeant of Colonel Henry O'Neill's Irish Regiment in Flanders in 1605. [WG]

ROSS, ROBERT, born 1710, an Irish Student at the University of Leiden in 1733.[UL]

ROSS, ROBERT, born in Dublin during 1766, son of Major David Ross of Rostrevor, County Down, was educated at Trinity College in Dublin, enrolled in the British Army, as a Major of the Twentieth Regiment of Foot he fought in the Low Countries where he was wounded at Krabbendam on 10 September 1799, also at Walcheren in August 1809. [TL.106]

ROUTH, ANDREW, a chaplain of Colonel James Dempsey's Irish Regiment in the Low Countries from 1660 until 1662. [WG]

ROYTER, CHARLES, born in 1620, master of the Mary of Antrim, a privateer, which was captured by the Tiger on 3 February 1649. [TNA.HCA.13.250]

ROWES, JOHN, from Ostend, Flanders, [Oostende, Vlaanderen] entered the service in Dunkirk, Duinkerken] of Captain Clement Van De Ryder, master of the privateer Cornelius of Wexford in October 1649. [TNA.HCA.13.250]

RUARKE, CORNELIUS, a Captain of Colonel Philip O'Reilly's Irish Regiment in the Low Countries from 1655 until 1660. [WG]

RUARKE, LAWRENCE, a Sergeant of Colonel John Morphy's Irish Regiment in Flanders from 1646 until 1659. [WG]

RUARKE, LAWRENCE, from Ostend, Flanders, [Oostende, Vlaanderen] entered the service at Dunkirk, of Captain Clement Van De Ryder, master of the privateer Cornelius of Wexford in October 1649. [TNA.HCA.13.250]

RUARKE, LAWRENCE, an Ensign of Colonel George Cusack's Regiment in the Low Countries from 1656 until 1662. [WG]

RUARKE, THADEUS, a Chaplain of Colonel Owen Roe O'Neill's Irish Regiment in Flanders from 1633 until 1642. [WG]

RUARKE, THADEUS, a Captain of Taafe's Irish Regiment in the Low Countries from 1672 until 1673; a Captain of Colonel Denis O'Byrne's Irish Regiment in the Low Countries from 1673 until 1686. [WG]

RUARKE, THOMAS, a Sergeant of Colonel Patrick O'Donnell's Irish Regiment in Flanders from 1643 to 1647. [WG]

RUBBENS, JACOB, was naturalised in Ireland on 6 February 1638. [IPR]

RUSSELL, BARTHOLEMEW, an Ensign of MacElligott's Regiment in Flanders in 1688. [IS]

RUSSEL, RICHARD, a Captain of Colonel George Cusack's Regiment in the Low Countries from 1656 until 1662; a Captain of Taafe's Irish Regiment in the Low Countries from 1672 until 1673; a Captain of Colonel Denis O'Byrne's Irish Regiment in the Low Countries from 1673 until 1686. [WG]

RYAN, CHARLES, a chaplain of Colonel Theodore's Irish Regiment in the Low Countries, 1660-1664. [WG]

RYAN, EDMOND, a soldier of Colonel Louis Farrell's Regiment in the Low Countries in 1660. [WG]

RYAN, JOHN, born 1723, an Irish student at the University of Leiden in 1746, [UL].

RYAN, LEWIS, Major of Colonel James Dempsey's Irish Regiment in the Low Countries from 1660 to 1662, and of Colonel John Murphy's Irish Regiment in the Low Countries from 1667 until 1669. [WG]

RYDER, CLEMENT, master of the Cornelius of Wexford, a Confederate privateer, brought three captured ships into Ostend in 1649. [TNA.HCA.13.250]

ST LEGER, ELIZABTH, born in the Netherlands, daughter of Sir William St Leger, was naturalised in Ireland on 27 April 1624. [IPR]

ST LEGER, WILLIAM, born in the Netherlands, son of Sir William St Leger, was naturalised in Ireland on 27 April 1624. [IPR]

SAMSON, JAN, from Limerick, was admitted as a citizen of Rotterdam on 26 May 1722. [RA]

SARSFELT, IGNATS, from Cork, was admitted as a citizen of Rotterdam on 11 December 1792. [RA]

SARSFIELD, PATRICK, was born at Lucan, County Dublin, son of Patrick Sarsfield of Lucan, he was educated at a French military college, then was an officer in Irish Regiments and fought at Limerick for King James in 1690, he then entered French service as Captain of the Irish Horse Guards, he was killed at the Battle of Landen in Flanders on 29 July 1693. [The Jacobite Peerage, Edinburgh, 1904]

SARSFIELD, PATRICK, a merchant from Doughchape, County Cork, based in Oostende [Ostend] letters from 1710 until 1755. [NLI]

SAVAGE, SENECA, a Captain of Colonel John Morphy's Irish Regiment in Flanders from 1646 until 1659. [WG]

SCHOULDAM, HELINOR, daughter of Edmond and Elizabeth Schouldam in Ship Street, Dublin, was baptised in St Bride's, Dublin, on 15 December 1709.

SEALE, ELIZABETH, born in 1622, of Ostend, Flanders, [Oostende, Vlaanderen] sailed from Waterford aboard the Angel Gabriel bound for France but storm-damaged put into Swansea in Wales in January 1650. [TNA.HCA.30]

SEALY, JOHN, born in 1706, an Irish student at the University of Leiden in 1726. [UL]

SENSARFE, GERALD, a mariner from Rotterdam, was naturalised in Ireland on 9 January 1663. [BL.Egerton.77]

SENSION, JACOB, born 1598, master of the Zoutketel van Vlissingen [Salt Kettle of Flushing] was captured in July 1646 by Captain Coachman master of the True Love when bound from Limerick. [TNA.HCA.13/60]

SHAA, JOHN, Captain of Colonel Louis Farrell's [formerly the Earl of Bristol's] Irish Regiment] bound for the Low Countries in 1658-1660 [WG]

SHAW, CHARLES, born in 1715, an Irish student at the University of Leiden in 1739. [UL]

SHEA, ANDREW, from Cork, was admitted as a citizen of Rotterdam on 15 April 1779. [RA]

SHEE, JOHN, from Dublin, married Maria Ann Galiem from Rotterdam, on 11 January 1711, in the City Church of Rotterdam. [RA]

SHERLE, EDWARD, Sergeant of Colonel Henry O'Neill's Irish Regiment in Flanders in 1605. [WG]

SHERLOCK, DAVID, born in 1699, an Irish student at the University of Leiden in December 1726. [UL]

SHEA, WALTER, a Captain of Colonel Thomas Preston's Irish Regiment in Flanders in 1773. [WG]

SHONNEL, WILLIAM, was born in Ireland in 1651, Captain of the Los Rios Regiment of Infantry, died in Brussels on 17 December 1753. [SM.15.581]

SHORTALL, THOMAS, born 1658 in Kilkenny, died in Landreci, Flanders, on 19 August 1762. He was Captain of Grace's Regiment at the Siege of Limerick in 1691, then with the remains of the Irish Army went to France. He was made a Knight of St Louis on 6 June 1729 and a Lieutenant Colonel in French Service on 10 June 1745 after the Battle of Fontenoy. [SM.24.567]

SICAN, JOHN, born in 1714, an Irish student at the University of Leiden in 1737. [UL]

SILVIUS, NATHANAEL, born 1660, an Irish student of medicine at the University of Leiden in 1686. [AH59]

SIMCOX, THOMAS, born in 1704, an Irish student at the University of Leiden in 1725. [UL]

SIMERELL, [Somerville?], WILLIAM, born 1612 in Scotland, master of the Paul of Rotterdam was bound from Amsterdam for Dublin, when taken by the Swanley an English man 'o War near Den Helder in 1648. [TNA.HCA.13.59]

SIMPSON, JOHN, born 1663, an Irish student at the University of Leiden in 1688. [UL]

SIMPSON, JOHN, born 1781, 'a visit to Flanders, chiefly the Field of Waterloo in 1815', died 1853. [NLI]

SINCLAIR, JOHN, born 1710, an Irish student at Leiden University in 1730. [UL]

SINGLETON, SAMUEL, born 1688, an Irish student at the University of Leiden in 1709. [UL]

SINOT, EDMOND, a Captain of Colonel Theodore O'Meara's Irish Regiment in the Low Countries from 1660 to 1664. [WG]

SKUES THOMAS, waiter aboard the Bonaventure of Vlissingen was imprisoned in Cork in 1665. [SPIre.1663-1665.]

SLABAERTE, ADRIAN, a merchant of Bruges, [Brugge], died 1606 in Tallaght, County Dublin.   [DPR.232] [NLI]

SLIEE, JOSEPH, from Cork, was admitted as a citizen of Rotterdam on 17 September 1720. [RA]

SLIGO, the Dowager Marchioness of, died in Amsterdam on 26 August 1817.   [SM.80.195]

SMALLEY, BENJAMIN, from Dublin, was admitted as a citizen of Rotterdam on 30 October 1720. [RA]

SMITH, ANDREW, born 1697, an Irish student at Leiden University in 1720. [UL]

SMITH, BENJAMIN, born 1684, an Irish student at Leiden University in 1704.   [AH.59]

SMITH, EDWARD, born 1708, an Irish student at Leiden University in 1729. [UL]

SMITH, HENRY, born in 1705, an Irish student at the University of Leiden in 1728,   an Irish academic at the University of Leiden in 1731. [UL]

SMITH, JAMES, from Ireland, married Annetge Broun from Ireland, on 9 January 1644 in the Reformed Church of Rotterdam. [RA]

SMITH, SAMUEL, born 1677, an Irish student at Leiden University in 1699. [AH.59]

SMITH, THOMAS, from Dublin, married Maria De Bruin from Yarmouth, on 17 January 1713 in the Reformed Church of Rotterdam. [RA]

SMYTH, BOYLE, born in 1742, an Irish student at the University of Leiden in 1742. [UL]

SNEBYE, GILBERT, born 1618, a mariner from Hamburg, aboard the Rowland of Bremen bound from La Rochelle for Wexford in 1643. [TNA.HCA.13.58]

85

SOULDERWAGHER, ADRIAN DIX, a mariner from Rotterdam, was naturalised in Ireland on 30 April 1669. [BL.Egerton.77][IPR]

SOUTHWELL, JAMES, born 1676, fought under the Duke of Marlborough at the Battle of Malplaquet in Spanish Flanders in 1709, died in Limerick on 10 November 1782. [SM.44.615]

SPRATT, JAMES, born in 1705, an Irish student at Leiden University in 1725, an Irish academic at the University of Leiden in 1728. [UL]

SPRINGER, JOHN CLAUSEN, a mariner from Howsduyn in Holland, was denisized in Ireland on 5 August 1675. [IPR]

SPREAD, NOBLET, born 1693, an Irish student at Leiden University in 1723. [UL]

STABEORT, KATHRIN, died 1597, daughter of Ludowick Stabeort in Bruges, wife of Thomas Molyneux, was buried in Christ Church in Dublin.

STAMFIELD, JAMES, son of Thomas Stamfield, in Londonderry, married Janet Gilmer, widow of A. Livingston, in the Scots Kirk of Rotterdam on 25 February 1711. [RA]

STANIHURST, JOHN, of Colonel Stanley's Regiment at Brussels in 1591. [AGRB.37]

STANIHURST, THOMAS, Captain of Colonel Henry O'Neill's Irish Regiment in Flanders in 1605. [WG]

STANLEY EDWARD, Captain of an Irish Regiment, sent to support the Dutch against the Spanish from 1586 until 1587 when the regiment changed allegiance in favour of Spain until 1604. [WG]; brother of Colonel William Stanley in 1591. [AGRB.38]

STANLEY, JOHN, formerly an Ensign of the disbanded company of Captain Edward Stanley in 1591. [AGRB.39]

STANLEY, MARTIN, of Drogheda, a passenger on board the <u>Fortune of Dunkirk</u> from Dunkirk bound for Ireland, in May 1643. [TNA.HCA.13.246.504]

STANLEY, WILLIAM, Colonel of an Irish Regiment, sent to support the Dutch against the Spanish from 1586 until 1587 when he changed allegiance in favour of Spain until 1604. [WG]

STAPBOARD, JOSEPH, born 1700, an Irish student at Leiden University in 1722. [UL]

STAPLETON, THEOBALD, born 1675, an Irish student at Leiden University in 1703. [AH.59]

STEWART, GILBERT, in Rotterdam, a letter to Lord Massareene, dated 10 September 1697. [PRONI.D562.16]

STRETCH, JOHN, born in 1713, an Irish student at the University of Leiden in 1743. [UL]

STRITCH, THOMAS, of Limerick, a passenger aboard the Fortune of Dunkirk from Dunkirk bound for Ireland in May 1643. [TNA.HCA.13.246.507]

STRONG, JOHN, waiter aboard the White Greyhound of Middelburg was imprisoned in Cork in 1665. [SPIre.1663-1665.665]

STRULTE, THEOPHILUS, loaded goods aboard the Blessing in Dublin in May 1645 for shipment to Isaac Paulson and Jacob Pankart in Holland. [TNA.HCA.13.58.167]

STUART, JOHN, born 1678, a Scots-Irish student at Leiden University in 1698. [AH.58]

STUART, WILLIAM, born 1714, an Irish student at the University of Leiden in 1735. [UL]

SULLIVAN, JOAN, from Cork, was admitted as a citizen of Rotterdam on 5 September 1719. [RA]

SUNDERVILLE, EDWARD, from Dublin, was admitted as a citizen of Rotterdam on 24 June 1710. [RA]

SWALF or SWAELOFF, JOSEPH, from Dublin, married Dorothea Driesen, from Doesburg, on 30 August 1729, later Johanna Kraemer, on 7 October 1749, in the Reformed Church of Rotterdam. [RA]

SWANLEY, RICHARD, master of the Leopard, captured the Pelikaan van Rotterdam in August 1644 when bound from Rotterdam to Dublin. [TNA.HCA.13/59.414]

SWARTSON, SWART, from Der Schelling in Holland, master of the Hope of Amsterdam, with a cargo of rye, was captured by John Rossiter, master of

87

an Irish man'o'war on 19 May 1648, then took the ship to Waterford. [TNA.HCA.13.61.279/281]

SWEEN, MAURICE, an Ensign of Colonel John Morphy's Irish Regiment in Flanders from 1646 until 1659. [WG]

SWEENEY, EDMOND, a Captain of Colonel John Morphy's Irish Regiment in Flanders from 1646 until 1659. [WG]

TAAFE, JOHN, a Captain of Colonel Denis O'Byrne's Irish Regiment in the Low Countries, from 1673 until 1686. [WG]

TAAFE, LUCAS, a Captain of Colonel Denis O'Byrne's Irish Regiment in the Low Countries from 1673 until 1686. [WG]

TAAFE, NICHOLAS, Colonel of an Irish Regiment in the Low Countries from 1672 until 1673. [WG]

TAF, PETER, a Captain of Colonel Patrick O'Donnell's Irish Regiment in Flanders from 1643 to 1647. [WG]

TAAFFE, Lord THEOBALD, born 1603, a Royalist who fought in the Wars of the Three Kingdoms, was sent to Brussels in 1650, Colonel of the Duke of Gloucester's Regiment in the Spanish Netherlands in 1656, a member of King Charles II 's court in exile in the Netherlands in 1660s, died in 1677.

TAAFE. THOMAS, Lieutenant Colonel of Nicholas Taafe's Irish Regiment in the Low Countries from 1672 until his death in 1673. [WG]

TALBOT, FRANCIS, an Ensign of Colonel Hugh O'Donnell's Regiment in Flanders from 1632 until 1638, a Captain of Colonel Thomas Preston's Irish Regiment in Flanders from 1634 until 1641. [WG]

TALBOT, GILBERT, Major of Colonel Charles Dillon's Regiment bound for Flanders in 1653. [WG]

TALBOT, THOMAS, a Captain of Colonel Thomas Preston's Irish Regiment in Flanders from 1634 until 1641. [WG]

TAYLOR, JAMES, from Londonderry, was admitted as a citizen of Rotterdam on 24 March 1789. [RA]

TAYLOR, PATRICK, a Captain of Colonel Thomas Preston's Irish Regiment in Flanders from 1634 until 1641, a Captain of Colonel Patrick O'Donnell's Irish Regiment in Flanders from 1643 to 1647. [WG]

TAYLOR, ROBERT, from Dublin, married Eva Aikman from Rotterdam, in the Scots Kirk in Rotterdam on 27 December 1738. [RA]

TEAGAN, JAMES, from Dublin, was admitted as a citizen of Rotterdam on 19 September 1739. [RA]

TERRY, JAMES, born 1722, an Irish student at the University of Leiden in 1746. [UL]

TERREL, RICHARD, a Captain of Colonel Owen Roe O'Neill's Irish Regiment in Flanders from 1633 until 1642. [WG]

THAUBIN, [Tobin?] RICHARD, from Ireland, married Susanna Houkraft Frosluis, in the Sluys in Flanders, on 25 September 1652 in the Reformed Church of Rotterdam. [RA]

THEREMEN, CORNELIUS, from Rotterdam, master of the Pieter van Rotterdam [Peter of Amsterdam], with a cargo of rye, was captured in March 1648 by John Rossitor, master of the Mary and John of Wexford when bound from Rotterdam to Bristol in May 1648. [TNA.HCA13.61.109/278/279]

THOMSON, LEWIS, a merchant in Belfast, owner of the cargo on board of the Brown Horse of Wodvey, near Hoorne in Holland, was captured by John Duff, master of the King Charles of Glasgow in 1628. [NRS.HCAS.AC7.1]

THOMSON, LEWIS, from Flanders or the Netherlands, a member of the Church of Ireland, was a burgess of Belfast from 1678 until 1708. [BMF]

THOMSEN, MICHAEL, in St Petersburg, Russia, a letter in Dutch to Isaac MacCartney, Alexander Stewart, James McClure, John Gordon and John Wallace merchants in Belfast, mentions John Polman in Narva, Russia dated 6 February 1726. [PRONI.D654.B.2.41]

THUNERMANS, CORNELIUS, master of the Peter of Rotterdam was seized by an Irish man-of-war in 1647. [TNA.HCA.15.5.882/883]

THWAITES, EPHRAIM, born 1694, an Irish student at Leiden University in 1714. [UL]

THYS, JAN, from Ireland, married ......from England, on 29 October 1636 in the Reformed Church of Rotterdam. [RA]

TIER, JOSEPH, from Dublin, married Magdaleenje van Spal from Hellevoetsluis, in the Reformed Church in Rotterdam on 9 August 1740. [RA]

TORELLA, DOMINICK MERRIMAN, a Captain of Colonel Dermot O'Sullivan's Irish Regiment in Flanders, from 1646 until 1647; a Captain of Colonel John Morphy's Irish Regiment in Flanders from 1646 until 1659. [WG]

TORQUIL, JOHN, Captain of Colonel Henry O'Neill's Irish Regiment in Flanders in 1605. [WG]

TRIMBLE, FRANCIS, from Dublin, was admitted as a citizen of Rotterdam on 25 August 1716; he married Jacoba Green from Rotterdam on 4 December 1718, in the Presbyterian Church in Rotterdam; in Rotterdam, a letter to A. Stewart and Company, dated 16 April 1726. [PRONI.D654.B2.50]

TROTTER, GERARD, from Enniskillen, in County Fermanagh, was admitted as a citizen of Rotterdam on 7 July 1759. [RA]

TUCKER, TIMOTHY, born 1693, an Irish student at Leiden University in 1723. [UL]

TUCKER, Captain of the 27th [Inniskilling] Regiment, fought at the Battle of Waterloo in 1815.

TUIT, GASPAR, a Captain of [formerly the Earl of Bristol's] Colonel Louis Farrell's Irish Regiment bound for the Low Countries in 1658-1660 [WG]

TULLY, CHARLES, a chaplain of Colonel James Dempsey's Irish Regiment in the Low Countries from 1660 until 1662. [WG]

TUCKER, TIMOTHY, born 1693, an Irish student at Leiden University in 1723. [UL]

TULLY, JOHN, from Ireland, marred Neeltje, widow of Jan Robbertz, in the Reformed Church in Rotterdam on 24 March 1654. [RA]

TURNER, CHRISTOPHER, born 1603, from Wexford, master of the Margaret of Wexford bound from Wexford with a cargo of herring and raw hides for Landorne in France, on 17 January 1643, but was captured by the Lily master John Lambert. TNA.HCA.13.246/503]

UNDERMARKE, Captain ANTONIO, born 1619, from Flanders, master of the Mary of Antrim with a commission from Viscount Muskerry the High Admiral of Ireland, caught several English ships and a Dutch one but was captured by the Tiger the taken to Plymouth. Mary of Antrim had a crew of 109 men, mostly Irish , Dutch and Dunkirkers also one Englishman. [TNA.HCA.13.250]

URIACHS, JOHN, born 1710, an Irish Student at the University of Leiden in 1732. [UL]

VAUGHAN, HECTOR, born 1701, an Irish student at Leiden University in 1724. [UL]

VAN CILSEL, refence to in will of Abel De Le Deveze, probate 1749. [PCC]

VAN DALE, JOHN, from Brabant, was granted denizisation in Ireland, on 7 June 1605. [IPR]

VAN DER RYDER, CLEMENT, master of the privateer Cornelius of Wexford which was captured by the Parliamentary ship the Tiger in November 1649. [TNA.HCA.13.850]

VAN ECKLINYSEN, GERRIT, reference to in will of Abel De Le Deveze, in 1749. [PCC]

VAN KASTEEL, JORIS from Dublin, married Agnietje Vlamings, from Solingen, in the Reformed Church in Rotterdam on 6 October 1705. [RA]

VAN DE LEUR, FRANCES, in Dublin, married William Boyle, a barrister at law, in 1766. [FDJ.4084]

VAN DE LEUR, FRANCIS, third son of James Van De Leur, a clerk in County Clare, referred to in his will dated 1729, Dublin.

VAN DE LEUR, HENRY, eldest son of James Van De Leur, a clerk in County Clare, referred to in his will dated 1729, Dublin.

VAN DE LEUR, JAMES, in Cork, probate 1667

VAN DE LEUR, JAMES, a clerk in County Clare, probate 1729, Dublin.

VAN DER LEUR, JOHN, an alderman of Cork in 1662. [CSPIre]

VAN DE LEUR, JOHN ORMSBY, born in 1767, Lieutenant Colonel of the 5th Dragoon Guards, died in Bristol, England, on 3 December 1822. [SM.89.752]

VAN DER LURE, FRANCIS, supplied drugs for the Army in Ireland in 1646. [SPIre.1633-1647.445]

VAN DE LURE, JAMES, in Cork, probate 1667, Diocese of Cork and Ross.

VAN DE LURE, JAMES, from Middelburg in Zealand, a resident of Cork, was naturalised in Cork on 1 September 1663. [IPR]

VAN DE LEUR, Reverend JAMES, in Cragg, County Clare, probate?, 1753, Diocese of Killaloe and Kilfenora.

VAN DE RYDER, CLEMENT, master of the Cornelius of Wexford, a privateer, recruited seamen in Dunkirk in October 1649, including Peter de Lard, a Fleming residing in Waterford, John Rowes from Ostend, Andreas Lye a Walloon from Douai, and Edmond Duff from Ireland, to attack English ships. On 2 November 1649 the Cornelius was captured by Captain Peacock of the Tiger and taken to Yarmouth. [TNA.HCA.13.250.665]

VAN DE WATER, SIBERT, a cooper born in Dordrecht in Holland was denizised in Ireland on 17 February 1668. [IPR]

VAN DER BEGGE, JAMES, from the Netherlands, was granted denizisation in Ireland on 22 March 1639. [IPR]

VAN DER HOULT, JOHN, was naturalised in Ireland on 28 May 1639. [IPR]

VAN DER KIPP, ..., master of the St Francis captured the William of London in April 1643 and sold it to .... Cheevers of Wexford. [MM.76.122]

VAN DER LURE, JOHN, an Alderman of Cork, 10 January 1662. [SPIre.16601662.496]

VAN DER MARCHE, ANTHONY, captain of the Mary of Antrim in November 1648, was granted letters of marque authorising him to be a privateer at sea attacking the enemies of Catholicism in Ireland and opponents of King Charles I. [MM.76.121]; captured the Prize, master Mark Fawson, and another ship, master Cornelius Baldon in 1648. [TNA.HCA.13.250.i]

VAN DER MERE, JOHN, at Red House, Sycamore Avenue, Dublin {?}, reference in the will of Daniel Malone, dated 1 November 1735, Dublin.

VAN DE RYDER, Captain CLEMENT, master of the Cornelius of Wexford was granted letters of marque to act against enemies of the king, on 9 July 1649. He captured the Barbars of Wells, master William Cuertis, in October 1649, and was bound with the Barbara for Dunkirk hen it was liberated by Captain Peacock and HMS Tiger and taken to Yarmouth. [TNA.HCA.13.250.1/666]

VAN DE W.....BERT, a cooper from Dordrecht in Holland, was naturalised in Ireland on 17 February 1667. [BL.Egerton.77]

VAN DER BEGGE, JAMES, from the Netherlands, was granted denizisation in Ireland on 22 March 1639. [IPR]

VAN DER CRUYS, ALPHONSE, at the Mill Bridge of Brugge, a letter from John, the Bishop of Derry dated 25 March 1653. [SPIre.1953.392]

VAN DER LENDY, FRANCIS, a merchant in Amsterdam trading with Limerick in 1648, with goods for John Peterson in Galway. [TNA.HCA.13.249]

VAN DER LURE, JAMES, a clergyman between Killenesullagh and Kilfinbuan, County Clare, around 1650. [SPIre.1650.295]

VAN DER MARCHE, ANTONIO, born 1619, from Flanders, master of the Mary of Antrim in 1649, was tried as a Confederate privateer, his crew of 109 men were Irish, Dutch or from Dunkirk. [TNA.HCA.13.250.1]

VAN DER MERE, HENRY, a painter and a publican in Angelsea Street, Dublin, died in 1764. [FDJ.3838]

VAN DER SEPEN, ANTHONY CLAUSON, of Wexford, part-owner of the Patrick of Waterford, a privateer, in 1647. [TNA.HCA.15.2]

VAN DER SHUREN, NICATUS, from the Netherlands, was granted denizisation in Ireland on 27 February 1635. [IPR]

VAN DER SIPE, ANTONIO NICHOLAS, owner of the St Francis in Waterford in 1647, which he sold to Marguerite de Namur wife of General Preston. [SPIre. 1633-1647.600]

VAN DER SIPE, MARTIN, brother of the above, in Waterford in 1647. [SPIre.1633-147.600]

VAN DER VOORT, ABRAHAM, from the Netherlands, was granted denizisation in Ireland on 27 February 1635. [IPR]

VAN DER VOORT, JOHN, from the Netherlands, was granted denizisation in Ireland on 27 February 1635. [IPR]; from Middleburg Zealand, with goods and an estate in Ireland, probate 1655, Prerogative Court of Canterbury [TNA]

VAN DOOREN, DANIEL, master of the privateer St John of Waterford sent five prize ships to Ostend in April and May 1649, was captured by Captain Coppin in the Greyhound in July 1649. [TNA.HCA.12.250, part ii]

VAN DUNDREIGHT, GERROT VAN ASPERIN, from the Netherlands, was granted denizisation in Ireland on 29 January 1620. [IPR]

VAN DICKE, ANN, daughter of Henry Dicke and his wife Elizabeth, in Ship Street, Dublin, was baptised in St Bride's, Dublin, on 24 October 1713.

VAN DIKE, HENRY, son of Henry Dike and his wife Elizabeth, in Ship Street, Dublin, was baptised in St Bride's, Dublin, on 13 June 1709.

VAN DIKE, HENRY, son of Henry van Dike and his wife Elizabeth, in Ship Street, Dublin, was baptised in St Bride's, Dublin, on 29 December 1711.

VAN DOOREN, DANIEL, from Duinkerken [Dunkirk], was master of the St John of Waterford in 1649. [TNA.HCA13.250]

VAN GELDER, Mr, a goldsmith, a warrant dated 31 May 1662. [SPIre.1660-1662.551]

VAN GUYNAM, BARTHOLOMEW, son of Cornelius Van Guynam, was baptised in St Bride's, Dublin, on 21 August 1670.

VAN HEEL, BARTHOLEMEW PIETERSON, master of the Oyster Hoyle of Rotterdam, shipped a cargo of tobacco etc to Galway for Oliver French a merchant there in 1648. [TNA.HCA.30.855]

VAN HELMONT, Dr., in Dublin in 1670. [SPIre.1669-1670, 322]

VAN HEMSKERKE, a Dutch Admiral, was shipwrecked off the Blasquet Islands in September 1669. [SPIre.1669-1670.274]

VAN HOBART, JAMES, a merchant from Germany, was denizised in Ireland on 22 May 1665. [IBR]

VAN HOGARDEN, ABRAHAM, a merchant from Holland was naturalised in Ireland on 27 January 1662. [BL.Egerton.77]; settled in Limerick, dead by 1666, partner of Laurence de Geer. [CSPIre.1663-1665.673]

VAN HOEGAERDEN, GEORGE, in Limerick, probate?, 1726, Diocese of Killaloe and Kilfenora.

VAN HOGARDEN, ISAAC, a merchant from Holland was naturalised in Ireland on 27 January 1662. [BL.Egerton.77]

VAN HOEGAERDEN, ISAAC, in Querrin, probate 1680, Diocese of Killaloe and Kilfenora.

VAN HOGARDEN, JACOB, a merchant from Holland was naturalised in Ireland on 27 January 1662. [BL.Egerton.77]

VAN HOGARDEN, PETER, a merchant from Holland was naturalised in Ireland on 27 January 1662. [BL.Egerton.77]

VAN HOLT,ADRIAN, a merchant from Dunkirk who settled in Wexford around 1640, sent a cargo of pipe staves aboard the Adventure of London, master Paul Dodd bound for San Lucar in Spain in 1643. [TNA.HCA.30.863.1159]

VAN HOLT, JAN PIETERS, master of the Bomvel van Amsterdam, was seized at Kinsale, when it arrived from Amsterdam in July 1649. [TNA.HCA.13/250]

VAN HOMRIGH, BARTHOLEMEW, a merchant from Amsterdam who settled in Dublin in 1681, letters in 1695. Formerly with Dehulter and Van Homrigh, merchant in Amsterdam, agents for merchant in Dublin. [TCD.750.428/2328] [BMF.181]

VAN H0MRIGH, ESTHER, daughter of Bartholemew Van Homrigh late of Dublin, probate 1723, Dublin.

VAN HOSSELL, Captain, in Dublin, in October 1665. [SPIre.1663-1665.654]

VAN HOVEN, GERRARD, from Amsterdam, Holland, was granted denizisation in Ireland on 5 March 1646. [Patent Rolls, 21 Car 1.14]; Garrett Van Hoven loaded goods aboard the Blessing in Dublin in May 1645 for shipment to Isaac Paulson and Jacob Pankart in Holland. [TNA.HCA.13.58.167]

VAN LEEWEN, GEORGE, in Cork, probate 1758, Diocese of Cork and Ross.

VAN LEEUWEN, JOHN, born 1684, an Irish student at Leiden University in 1704. [AH.59]; a Dutch-Irish academic at Utrecht University in 1705. [UL]

VAN LEWEN, JOHN, a Doctor of Physics in Dublin, a witness to the will of William Webb in Garrane, County Limerick, dated 16 November 1722, Dublin.

VAN LEWEN, MEADE, born 1711, an Irish Student at the University of Leiden in 1735. [UL]

VAN LITH, HENRICK, a merchant from Dordrecht in Holland, was naturalised in Ireland on 17 February 1667. [BL.Egerton.77]

VAN NOLE, BARTHOLEMEW, master of the Oyster Hoyle of Rotterdam captured the Constant Warwick trading from Amsterdam to Galway in March 1648. [TNA.HCA.30.855.61]

VAN PERSIN, ADRIAN, refence to in will of Abel De Le Deveze, probate 1749, PCC. [TNA]

VAN PERSIN, Mrs Cornelia, refence to in will of Abel De Le Deveze, probate 1749, PCC. [TNA]

VAN PERSIN, COVERT, refence to in will of Abel De Le Deveze, probate 1749, PCC. [TNA]

VAN REEDE-GINKEL, GODARD ADRIAN, born 6 January 1621 in the Netherlands, a General during the Williamite Wars in Ireland, Commander in Chief of the British Forces there, 1st Earl of Athlone, died in Copenhagen, Denmark, during 1691.

VAN SOMEREN, ADRIAN GERETSEN, from Sardam in Holland, was permitted to go to Ireland to assess the possibility of Dutch families settling there, on 2 January 1662. [SPIre.1660-1662.500]

VAN STEELANT, ANNA, born 1634, daughter of John Van Steelant, residing in Waterford in by 1651. [TNA.HCA.13.25]

VAN STEELANT, JOHN, born 1611, a merchant from Waterford, later in the Scilly Islands, trading with St Malo or Jersey in 1651. [TNA.HCA.13.255]

VAN STITTART, ARTHUR, married the sister of Lord Coleraine on 2 August 1773. [SM.35.445]

VAN STON, THOMAS, probate 1786, Cloyne.

VAN SWINDON, PHILIP, chairmaker and upholster, died in Moor Street, Dublin, in 1765. [FDJ.3934]

VAN TREIGHT, GEORGE, in Kilkenny, probate 1765, Ossory

VAN TREIGHT, WALTER, a limner [painter] in Kilkenny, was denizised in Ireland on 5 October 1699.

VAN TREAT, WALTER, referred to in the will of Nicholas Rohd in St Mary's, Dublin, dated 22 April 1708 in Dublin.

VAN UFFLE, Captain PATRICK, on board the frigate Dartmouth at Milford Haven, Wales, bound for Waterford in September 1665. [SPIre]

VAN VOOREN, DANIEL, master of the St John of Waterford in 1648. [TNA.HCA .13.250]

VAN WOODSWYK, CONST., reference to in will of Abel de le Deveze in 1749. [PCC]

VAN WAIEMOUTH, Captain John Peters, master of the frigate Mary of Ulster, a privateer in the service of the Irish Catholic Confederates, captured the Mary of Amsterdam in 1648. [TNA.HCA.30.549]

VAN WEEDE, CORNELIS, a factor or merchant in Belfast who returned to the Netherlands by 1675. [CSP.Ire.1669-1670.321]; [TNA.C114.77/76/72]

VAN YZENDOOLEN, HERMAN, in Rotterdam, a letter to Daniel Mussenden in Belfast on 15 July 1755. [PRONI.D354.622]

VARILLA, JOHN, from Vlissingen, Zealand, was denizised in Ireland on 7 July 1623. [IPR]

VAUGHAN, FRANCIS, born 1666, an Irish student at the University of Leiden in 1688. [AH59]

VER BRAKEN, ROWLAND, in Kilkenny, probate, 1680, Diocese of Ossory.

VERBURG, JEREMIAS, from Cork, married Pieternellje Franse, from Delfhaven, in the Reformed Church in Rotterdam on 30 October 1714. [RA]

VERDOEN, PIETER MARTYN, from Dublin, married Hendrina De Heus, from Rotterdam, in the Reformed Church in Rotterdam on 28 April 1735; was admitted as a citizen of Rotterdam on 1 October 1736. [RA]

VERDON, CHRISTOPHER, in County Louth, on 18 March 1625. [CSPIre.i.86]

VERDON, HENRY, in Cork, a will in 1572.

VERDON, HENRY, in Cork, a will in 1638.

VERDON, WILLIAM, in Cork, a will in 1571.

VERDON, HENRY, in Ballintober, will in 1713.

VERELST, DICK, refence to in will of Abel De Le Deveze, probate 1749, PCC. [TNA]

VERELST, SARAH, refence to in will of Abel De Le Deveze, probate 1749, PCC. [TNA]

VERELST, Mrs, reference to in will of Abel De Le Deveze, probate 1749, PCC. [TNA]

VEREKER, GEORGINA, married J.F. Hamilton of Westport in Limerick on 2 August 1817. [SM.80.97]

VEREKER, JOHN, an Alderman of Limerick, probate 1789, Limerick

VERHOVEN, GERALD, from Antwerpen, Flanders, was denizised in Ireland on 18 June 1605. [IPR]

VERHOVEN, JOHN, from Brabant, was denizised in Ireland on 7 June 1605. [IPR]

VERHOVEN, DERRICK HUBERT, a merchant from Dordrecht in Holland, was denizised in Ireland on 6 September 1608. [IPR]

VERIDET, JONATHAN, reference to in will of Jonathan de Lostal in Dublin, probate 1749, PCC. [TNA]

VER LIN, ELLINOR, in Cork, probate 1735, Diocese of Cork and Ross.

VERLIN, THOMAS, in Ballybreen, County Clare, probate, 1779. Diocese of Killaloe and Ross.

VERLING, DAVID, in Cork, probate, 1747. Diocese of Killaloe and Ross.

VERLING, JOHN, in Ballydeloghie, probate, 1733. Diocese of Killaloe and Ross.

VERLING, NICHOLAS, of Carrigiline, probate, 1697. Diocese of Killaloe and Ross.

VERLING, THOMAS, in Cork, probate, 1744. Diocese of Killaloe and Ross

VER LOO, ROBERT, from Belfast, was admitted as a citizen of Rotterdam on 18 September 1773. [RA]

VER TUIEL, Mrs, reference to in will of Jonathan de Lostal in Dublin, probate 1749, PCC. [TNA]

VERVEER, Sir HUBERT ADRIEN, Lord Mayor of Dublin in 1661. [SPIre.1660-1662.346]

VINCENT, HENDRIK, from Dublin, married Sandrina Langlois from Arnhem, in the Reformed Church in Rotterdam on 8 December 1709. [RA]

WAARTS, THOMAS, from Dublin, married Henrietta van der Heyl from Rotterdam in the Reformed Church there on 4 November 1703. [RA]

WADDEN, PATRICK, master of the John of Wexford, a privateer, which was active off the coast of Scotland, among his captures was a Scottish ship which had brought 8,000 [!] Danish soldiers to Scotland, later he captured ships with cargoes of salt that were taken to Wexford by 1649. [TNA.HCA.13.250.835]

WADDING, PETER, born around 1581, from Waterford, Professor of Theology in Antwerp, Prague and Graz, died in 1644. [DPR.38]

WADDING, WILLIAM, master of the Mary and Joseph was granted Letters of Marque by the Irish Confederate Council in 1646; master of the Catherine of Wexford, 90 tons, partly owned by the master and partly by John Talbot in Wexford, sailed from Waterford in 1648 with cargo of herring, butter, tallow, wool, and frieze sent by merchants John White, James, Lanthorne, and Nicholas Lee bound for William Lee an Irish merchant in La Rochelle, then from there with a cargo, sent by William Lee, consisting of salt, wine, aqua vita, liquorice and biscuits on 19 January 1649 bound for Waterford. The Catherine was captured by Captain Penn master of the Assurance, off Dursey Island on 25 January 1649. [TNA.HCA.15.5.906]

WAESBERGH, PETER, a merchant from Rotterdam, was naturalised in Ireland on 19 July 1665. [BL.Egerton.77][IPR]

WAGGYN, PHILIP, from Dublin, married Achje Ariens, in the Reformed Church in Rotterdam on 4 February 1601. [RA]

WALKER, WILLIAM, from Dublin, married Jane Shipley from Rotterdam, in the Episcopalian Church there on 19 April 1783; he was admitted as a citizen of Rotterdam on 13 April 1783. [RA]

WALS, JAN, from Ireland, married Margarita Jans from Antwerpen, in the Reformed Church of Rotterdam on 1 April 1635. [RA]

WALSH, Captain LUCAS, a memorandum of service, he was an Ensign in the Duke of York's Regiment until 1657, then to the Low Countries to fight the French, Walsh was captured at the Siege of Dunkirk in 1658, he was ransomed then was sent to serve in Spain, from there to London at the Restoration, in October 1660 he became commander of the frigate Assurance, later he was captain of the Grace of Dublin, a man of war, and fought the Dutch, the French and the Danes, a petition dated 1668. [SPIre]

WALSH, JAMES, an Ensign of Colonel Theodore's Irish Regiment in the Low Countries, 1660-1664. [WG]

WALSH, JOHN, from Waterford, was admitted as a citizen of Rotterdam on 19 September 1769. [RA]

WALSH, PETER, a Catholic priest in Flanders, was permitted to recruit 4000 Irishmen to serve the King of Spain on 26 May 1653. [IPC.II.343]

WALSH, Colonel PIERSE, left Ireland in 1652 to serve the Royal cause abroad, he served in the Duke of Ormond's regiment in Flanders, petitioned King Charles II in 1661. [CSPIre]

WALSH, THOMAS, from Waterford, was admitted as a citizen of Rotterdam on 10 November 1793. [RA]

WALSH, VALENTINE, an Ensign of MacElligott's Regiment in Flanders in 1688. [IS]

WALTER, FRANCIS, born in Limerick, a merchant in Spain, Germany, Zealand, Amsterdam, and in 1653 in London. [TNA.HCA.13.68]

WANING, WESTERNRA, from Dublin, was admitted as a citizen of Rotterdam on 5 August 1719. [RA]

WARD, WILLIAM, formerly a Captain in Colonel Stanley's Regiment in 1591. [AGRB.42]

WARREN, HENRY, born 1690, an Irish student at the University of Leiden in 1713. [UL]

WARREN, Captain JAMES, died at Grange, County, Kilkenny, on 24 December 1757, he served under the Duke of Marlborough, and was at the Battles of Huchslet, Malplaquet, and at the Sieges of Lisle, Douai, and Ghent, also was at the Battle of Sheriffmuir in 1715. [SM.20.51]

WARREN, LEMUEL, born 1771 in Dublin, an officer of the 27th [Inniskilling] Regiment, served in Flanders from 1793 until 1795, and in the West Indies in 1796, he died as a Major General in London in 1833.

WATTS, WILLIAM, a merchant in Dublin, trading with Antwerpen and Ostende in Flanders, in 1666. He along with Francos Kniffe and Alexander De Schodt, merchants in Antwerpen, loaded the St Francis van Antwerpen with merchandise bound for Ireland but was shipwrecked off Portpatrick, Scotland. [NRS.RH9.3.51]

WECKES, WILLIAM, born 1699, an Irish student at Leiden University in 1719. [UL]

WEESTER, JACOB DERRICKSON, born 1613, master of the St Jacob of Middelburg from there with a cargo of rye bound for Waterford in 1649. [TNA.HCA.13.61.312]

WELLEY, THOMAS, from Londonderry, married Annetje Kuyken, widow of Dirk Domen, from Rotterdam. In the Reformed Church there on 23 November 1706. [RA]

WELLS, THOMAS, Captain of the Catt, a privateer, captured the Middelburg of Middelburg of Zealand near the mouth of the River Shannon bound for Limerick in 1647. [TNA.HCA.13/62]

WESLEY, EDMOND, of Colonel Stanley's Regiment, was permitted to return to Ireland in 1591. [AGRB.46]

WESTENRA, ARNOLD, from Campen, Overrijssel, in Holland, was denizised in Ireland on 5 March 1646. [IPR]

WESTENRA, DERICKE, from Campen, Oversillis, Holland, a merchant in Ireland, also his sons Pieter and Warner, were granted denizisation in Ireland in 1640, and naturalisation on 22 November 1655. [Patent Roll, Commonwealth, 1.3/29]; 1662 [14-15. Car.ii]

WESTENRA, WARNER, from Haarlem, Holland, was denizised in Ireland on 22 November 1655, [Patent Roll, Commonwealth.1.3/29]; a merchant who was granted naturalisation in Ireland in 1662. [14-15 Car.ii]

WESTENRA, ..., a merchant of the Canary Company in 1666. [SPIre]

WESTON, WILLIAM, a Captain of Colonel John Morphy's Irish Regiment in Flanders from 1646 until 1659. [WG]

WESTROP, MICHAEL BUSTEED, in Cork, probate 1791, Cork.

WESTROP, RUDOLPH, born in Cork in 1717, an Irish student at the University of Leiden in 1739. [UL]

WHITAKER, WILLIAM, an Irish academic at the University of Leiden in 1718. [UL]

WHITE, FRANCIS, of Limerick, a passenger aboard the <u>Fortune of Dunkirk</u> from Dunkirk bound for Ireland in May 1643. [TNA.HCA.13.246.510]

WHITE, JAMES, an Irish soldier in the company of Colonel William Stanley in 1588. [AGRB.8]

WHYTE, MICHAEL, a Captain of Colonel John Morphy's Irish Regiment in Flanders from 1646 until 1659. [WG]

WHITE, NICHOLAS, Captain of MacElligott's Regiment in Flanders around 1688. [IS]

WHITE, THOMAS, born 1705, an Irish Student at the University of Leiden in 1735. [UL]

WHITTLE, JOHN, born 1700, an Irish student at Leiden University in 1712. [UL]

WILLIAMS, GRIETGE, from Ireland, married Hendry Hendry, a soldier from Orkney, Scotland, in Rotterdam on 26 March 1606. [RA]

WILLIAMSON, DOMINIC, a merchant from Vlissingen in Holland, was naturalised in Ireland on 12 October 1669. [BL.Egerton.77] [IPR]

WILLIAMSON, JOHN, born 1690, an Irish student at the University of Leiden in 1713. [UL]

WILLS, DAVID, from Waterford, married Alida Ver Boom from Rotterdam, in the Reformed Church there on 7 October 1732. [RA]

WILLS, JOHN, master of the Elizabeth of Limerick from Limerick to Dunkirk in Flanders and return in 1642. [TNA.HCA.30.840]

WINDSOR, FRANCIS, a gentleman from the Netherlands, was granted denization in Ireland on 9 June 1626. [IPR]

WOOD, GEORGE, from Belfast, married Jane Ross from Orkney, in the Scots Kirk in Rotterdam on 19 November 1704. [RA]

WOUTERSZ., BARENT, from Dublin, married Amerensje Barents, from Oud Bierland, in the Reformed Church in Rotterdam on 28 March 1677. [RA]

WYBRANTS, DANIEL, a native of Holland, was denizised in Ireland on 7 January 1624. [IPR]; a merchant of the Canary Company, petitioned King Charles II in July 1666. [SPIre]

WYBRANTS, DANIEL, senior, an Alderman of Dublin, a Dutch subject, who was naturalised in Ireland, along with his wife Elizabeth, and children including his sons Daniel junior, Peter, and Henry. However, Daniel senior died in Holland before 1673 and Henry, however Daniel senior died in Holland before 1673. [SPDom.1673.500]

WYBRANTS, PIETER, a merchant in Dublin, a deed in 1631. [ONA.Rotterdam.42.109/172]

WYBRANT, PETER, an Alderman of Dublin in 1662-1663. [SPIre.1663-1665.78/499]; a merchant of the Canary Company in 1666, [SPIre]; he loaded goods aboard the Blessing in Dublin in May 1645 for shipment to Isaac Paulson and Jacob Pankart in Holland. [TNA.HCA.13.58.167] a Commissioner of Appeal in 1668, [SPIre]; a magistrate in 1684.

YITON {AYTON?}, ROBERT, born 1669, a Scots-Irish student at the University of Leiden in 1693. [UL]

SUPPLEMENTS

TRANSATLANTIC VOYAGES

BORDEAUX OF FLUSHING, master Claus Clausen, from Flushing in the Netherlands, bound for La Rochelle, from there with a cargo of tobacco, brandy and wine sailed to the West Indies, traded in St Eustatius and Martinique, and then was bound for Holland but the destination was changed to Waterford, however the ship being storm damaged it put into Glendore, Ireland, in 1647. [TNA.HCA.13.248]

BORDEAUX OF VEERE, master John Cornelison, sailed from Middelburg on 16 May 1646, via La Rochelle bound for the West Indies, returned bound for Zeeland but was forced through storm damage to land at Glendore in Ireland in 1647. [TNA.HCA.13.62]

FLORA OF AMSTERDAM, master Cornelius Howers, from St Michael's in the West Indies with a cargo of sugar bound for Amsterdam, arrived in Dingle, Ireland in 1646. [TNA.HCA.13.248]

SAINT MARIA OF AMSTERDAM, master Cornelius Garbruntson, from St Kitts and Antigua bound for the Netherlands, forced by the weather to put into Galway in 1653. [TNA.HCA.13.67]

IRELAND AND THE PRIVATEERS

ADVENTURE, Captain Rogers, from Memel bound for Limerick was captured by the French in 1782. [SM.44.220]

AMAZON, George Colville, master of the privateer Amazon which was wrecked near Bangor on 25 February 1780. [Bangor Abbey gravestone]

ELIZABETH OF LIMERICK, when bound from Dunkirk to Limerick, was captured and taken to Falmouth in England in December 1641. [TNA.13.58.20]

GRACE OF DUNDEE, master William, Halliburton, born 1601, a mariner from Dundee, aboard the Grace of Dundee with a cargo of pilchards, bound from Bantry, Ireland, for Villefranche was captured by French warships and taken to Toulon in January 1629. [TNA.HCA.13.48.767]

DILIGENCE OF DUBLIN, 120 tons, master Andew Middleton, when homeward bound with a cargo of brandy, was captured by a privateer in 1707. [NRS.GD220.6.1743]

DUNGARVAN, a frigate and privateer, in 1643. [TCD.ms820.298]

ELIZABETH OF LIMERICK, was captured in December 1641, when bound from Dunkirk to Limerick

FRANCIS OF WEXFORD, master Thomas White, a privateer, 16 guns, captured the Mary and Dorothy of London in 1644. [TNA.HCA13.59]

GIFT OF GOD OF ABERDEEN, master Thomas Boyes, when bound from Aberdeen to Veere in the Netherlands in June 1639, was captured by an Irish frigate and taken to Ireland. [ACL.2.378][ABR.28.9.1643]

HARE OF WEXFORD, 50 tons, 6 guns, 40 crew, a privateer, Captains Stafford and Roche in 1643-1644. [TNA.HCA.30.849.552] [TCD.256.ms819]

MARGARET AND ELIZABETH OF WATERFORD, master Jacob Peararfiut, was captured by Parliamentary forces in 1649. [TNA.HCA.3.232]

MARY OF ANTRIM, a privateer, master Anthony Van Der Marche, captured the Prize master Mark Fawson and master Cornelius Baldon, in September 1648. [TNA]

MARY AND JOHN OF WEXFORD, a privateer, 16 guns, 160 crew, Captain John Rossitor, captured the Jonathan of Southampton when bound from Barbados to England in 1647.

MARY VIRGIN OF WEXFORD, master William O'Dorran, a privateer, seized the Peter of London bound from Galicia with a cargo of oranges for London in January 1649. [TNA.HCA.13.250]

PATRICK OF WATERFORD, master Wiliam Hayes, was captured when bound to Dublin in January 1642.

PATRICK OF WATERFORD, a privateer, 6 guns, Captain Francis Oliver, was captured by the Adventure, 32 guns, Captain Bedell, in 1647. [TNA.HCA.15.2]

PILGRIM also the CICERO, privateers under Hugh Hill, born in Carrickfergus, Ireland in 1740, settled in Beverley, Massachusetts, fought as a privateer during the Revolutionary War.

SAINT FRANCIS captured the Adventure of London, master Paul Dodd, with a cargo of sugar, which was taken to Wexford in 1643. [TNA.HCA.13.58.603]

SAINT JOHN OF WATERFORD, master Daniel Van Dooren, 5 guns, sent five captured ships bound to Ostend, Flanders, in April and May of 1649, [TNA.UCA.13.250]; it was seized by the Greyhound in 1649. [IWS.133]

SAINT PATRICK OF WEXFORD, a privateer, Captains Pruneas and Hayes, in July 1643; [TNA.HCA.13.58.603][IWS.133]

SAINT PETER OF WATERFORD a privateer, Captain Joseph Constant in April 1649. [TNA.HCA.30.855.202]

SWALLOW OF YOUGHAL, master Walter Quint, was captured by Parliamentary forces when bound from Youghal to Bristol in England, in 1644. [TNA.HCA.13246]

.......OF ABERDEEN, master George Aikman, was captured by an Irish frigate in November 1639. [ACL.3.131] [JCC241]

SOME PRIZES OF THE PRIVATEERS

The Peter of Helvoetsluis, a prize ship sold in Ireland for £136 in 1666.

The King David of Amsterdam, a prize ship, sold in Ireland for £200 in 1666.

The cargo of the Orange Tree sold in Ireland for £140 in 1666.

The White Greyhound of Middelburg, a prize ship, sold for £260 in July 1665.

The Bonaventure of Vlissingen, a prize ship, sold in Kinsale for £200 in July 1665.

The Mercurius of Vlissingen, a prize ship, sold in Kinsale for £430 in July 1665.

NOTABLE PIRATES FROM IRELAND

BARRY, JOHN, born 1745 in County Wexford, emigrated to Philadelphia, Pennsylvania, in 1760, master of the Lexington on 14 March 1776, captured <u>HMS Edward</u> on 6 April 1776, master of the <u>Alliance</u> in the West Indies in 1782, sent to France in February 1781, on the return voyage captured two merchant vessels also <u>HMS Atlanta</u> and <u>HMS Trepanny,</u> later fought privateers and French ships in the West Indies. [TL]

BONNEY, ANNE, born in County Cork daughter of William Cormack, emigrated to South Carolina, married in 1718 to James Bonney a seaman, settled in New Providence, in the Bahamas, where she joined the pirate crew of Captain John Rackham, in 1720 she and others were captured and tried in Kingston, Jamaica. She was condemned to death but liberated her father and returned to South Carolina where she died on 25 April 1782. [TL.18]

RYAN, LUKE, born in Ireland, master of a privateer in American service, based at Duinkerken, [Dunkirk] during the American Revolutionary War, in 1779 aboard the <u>Black Prince</u> destroyed shipping off Argyll and attacked a village there, in 1780 aboard the privateer <u>Dreadnaught</u> 150 tons, he cruised off the coast of Scotland, capturing a whaler from Newcastle and a collier of Saltcoats in Ayrshire, as well as plundering villages in the Hebrides. On 3 May 1781 he was captured aboard the <u>Calonies Dunkerque</u> off Berwick by the Royal Navy, was sentenced to death on a charge of 'felony and piracy on the high seas' but was pardoned. [MHS][SM.43.278]